ForeclosureFriendlies.com

How Families Can Save Their Homes from Foreclosure and How Investors Can Profit by Helping

By
Rick Rogers, JD/MBA

ForeclosureFriendlies.com Copyright © 2019 by Rick Rogers. All Rights Reserved.

All rights reserved. No part of this book may be reproduced in any form or by any electronic or mechanical means including information storage and retrieval systems, without permission in writing from the author. The only exception is by a reviewer, who may quote short excerpts in a review.

Cover designed by Madeeha Shaikh

Visit my website at www.ForeclosureFriendlies.com

Printed in the United States of America

First Printing: Jan 2019
Kindle Direct Publishing

ISBN-13 978-0-578-43542-8

This book is dedicated to Katie-Lee Harrison, Margaret Cahill, and George Olsen. Absent the devotion and toil of these three compassionate souls, the crusade could never have been nearly as successful as it was. My sincere thanks to each of you!

Table of Contents

Introduction 9

    Important Considerations 12

    Definitions: 13

Chapter 1: A Brief History 17

    Discovering Real Estate 17

    Flipping Foreclosures 17

    Foreclosure Investment Hits Close to Home 18

    The 2008 Foreclosure Crisis 20

    The Rogers Law Group and the "Four Corner Defense" 20

    Red Lark and Beyond 21

Chapter 2: Conventional Foreclosures, Profits, & Lessons Learned 23

    Conventional Foreclosure Auctions 23

    Foreclosure Auction Lessons Learned: 26

    Estimating Profits on Conventional Foreclosure Auctions 28

Chapter 3: Foreclosure Friendlies in a Nutshell 33

    Conventional Foreclosure Investment v. the Friendly Foreclosure 33

    The Friendly Foreclosure Process 34

    A Friendly Foreclosure in its Simplest Form 35

Chapter 4: Foreclosure Friendly Flips and Holds 41

Example #1 – A Friendly Foreclosure Flip 41

Example #2 – Another Friendly Foreclosure Flip 45

Example #3 – A Friendly Foreclosure Hold........................ 49

Double Your Returns on Foreclosure Friendly Holds!........... 54

Leverage 57

Chapter 5: Qualifications of a Good Foreclosure Friendly Candidate 61

Are You a Premier Foreclosure Friendly? 61

The Premier Foreclosure Friendly... 70

Chapter 6: Determining and Negotiating Terms 75

The Lease with Rider.. 75

Terms of the Friendly Foreclosure Transaction 75

Documents and Pre-Auction Work to be Done by Investors 84

Chapter 7: Finding a Friendly Investor... 91

The Premier Investor 91

Important Message to Friendlies and Investors 95

How to Find a Friendly Foreclosure Investor 98

Chapter 8: Finding Foreclosure Friendlies 101

How to Find a Foreclosure Friendly 103

Chapter 9: ForeclosureFriendlies.com 109

Like Match.com for Friendlies & Investors 109

Chapter 10: The Amazing LIRP 113

Conclusion 117

POSTSCRIPT I – So, You Want to Invest in Real Estate?........ 119

POSTSCRIPT II – Yes, We Can Help You!............................. 125

POSTSCRIPT III – Bankers, Increase Foreclosure Recovery Revenue by Decreasing Auction Bids!.. 127

Acknowledgment 133

Index of Charts & Tables

Table 1 – Calculating Profit on a Finished Value of $100,000.. 27

Table 2 – Pre-Tax Comparison: "Three-Year Hold" and "Flip to After-Auction Buyer" 45

Table 3 – Terms of a Three-Year Hold with a Mortgage 47

Table 4 – Pre-Tax Analysis & Comparison of Three-Year Hold with and Without a Mortgage 48

Table 5 – Comparison: Calculating Profit - Friendly Foreclosure v. Conventional Foreclosure... 66-67

Sample Rider 72

Introduction

Welcome homeowners and investors!

If you're in foreclosure and want to keep your home, you bought the right book!

If you're an investor who would like to make dramatic real estate profits by helping homeowners keep their homes, you bought the right book!

The Friendly Foreclosure Strategy in its entirety is probably quite different than any other foreclosure investment strategy of which you've heard before. The ultimate goal is for homeowners and investors to work together and help each other reach a mutually beneficial outcome.

If you're an Investor, this book will provide you with an exciting, new investment strategy which will provide impressive monetary returns as well as a level of personal satisfaction and fulfillment not typically found in real estate investments. Investors, I hope you enjoy this book on your way to making a fortune while helping many good families save their homes.

If you are a homeowner and this strategy works for you, then you will be able to continue living in your home AFTER the foreclosure like you always have. No moving required! In fact, your children and neighbors won't know the difference. Your family will continue to live in the home, uninterrupted, taking care of it, and treating it like your own. The hope and intention of the program are that one day it will again become your own. I've seen it work firsthand in amazing ways, and it may work as well or better for you!

> *If you turn out to be a good Foreclosure Friendly candidate, you may be in high demand. Investors may display great interest in helping you keep your home. No, they won't just be interested in buying your home at a discount for themselves. They'll sincerely want to help you keep it! That will be the most rewarding result for you AND those investors who understand this strategy.*

ForeclosureFriendlies.com? Is that a book or a website? Yes, as you may have guessed, it's both. This book will lay out the process and explain the benefits to homeowners and investors. The companion website, also titled ForeclosureFriendlies.com, is like the Match.com of homeowners in foreclosure and the investors who want to help them. That's where many of you will go to find your Foreclosure Friendly matches after you understand the concepts explained in this book.

Over the years, many Investors have come to me seeking qualified homeowners in foreclosure, whom we call Foreclosure Friendlies, or just Friendlies. **Frankly, we've never had enough Friendlies to satisfy the strong investor demand. This book is a shout-out to you Friendlies! Investors need to know about you, so they can help you!** Moreover, if you're lucky enough to be a Premier Foreclosure Friendly, which requires some work and some luck, then investors may be clamoring to help you. As an investor, myself, I know I would be interested in talking to any Premier Foreclosure Friendly in Illinois.

> *Using the strategy divulged in this book, many homeowners in foreclosure across the country, with or without my further assistance, will have a fighting chance to save their home under financially attractive terms, even when all else has failed and their situation seems hopeless. I can't guarantee this book will save your home, but it can give you one last*

fighting chance. Most don't get that. I hope you'll take advantage of this opportunity.

 In addition to revealing the strategy to homeowners in need, I hope to popularize this strategy among investors. The benefits to investors are considerable, and there are far more qualified investors than qualified homeowners in foreclosure. The more popular this strategy becomes among investors, the more homes we will save.

Friendlies and Investors are both required players on the Friendly Foreclosure team, and both can benefit incredibly by mutually pursuing the strategy described in this book. If you can't find each other on your own, create a profile at ForeclosureFriendlies.com, and we'll try to help.

If completed as recommended herein, the results of a Friendly Foreclosure strategy should range from attractive to spectacular for the homeowner and the investor. Wherever you fall in that range, you'll either be saving your home or helping a nice family save theirs. Either would be an admirable result, in addition to the magnitude of the financial benefits.

Throughout this book, you'll see a homeowner icon where I address homeowners specifically, and an investor icon where I talk to investors specifically.

   Investors Icon

   Homeowners Icon (aka Friendly, or Friendlies)

For both groups, I urge you to read the entire book, so you'll know the process for both sides.

Important Considerations

Names, locations, details, and figures used in this book were changed to simplify and preserve individual privacy. For financial alterations, I maintained the same percentage relationships, so the nature of the results would be unchanged.

Foreclosure laws vary from state to state. The examples in this book are based on Illinois mortgage foreclosure law and practice and should not be considered typical for any area outside of Illinois. I am not a CPA nor a Tax Advisor. Although I am a licensed attorney, nothing in this book nor responses or communications to readers is legal or tax advice. Consult your own attorney or tax advisor before utilizing any strategies described in this book.

Foreclosure auctions are generally open to the public, and there is always a risk that a friendly investor will lose at the auction. A homeowner seeking to save their home from foreclosure should first exhaust all other options, such as loan modification, foreclosure defense, mediation, and if applicable, bankruptcy.

Although the Foreclosure Friendly strategy may yield the best possible results, other conventional means may provide less risk and will no longer be available after a foreclosure auction. If those conventional alternatives fail, you'll still have a fighting chance to keep your home with the Foreclosure Friendly strategy. Good luck!

Definitions:

Friendly/Friendlies — homeowner(s) whose homes are in foreclosure and who want to keep their homes

Investors — those with the available resources and passion for helping homeowners while profiting from the underlying real estate transactions

Friendly Foreclosure strategy — the strategy that helps homeowners (Friendlies) who are in foreclosure stay in their homes with the help of an Investor.

Lease — a rental Contract between the new homeowner (in our strategy, the Investor), and the former homeowner living in the home

Purchase Option — a term that will generally be included in the lease wherein the family leasing the house will have the option to purchase the property within a certain timeframe in the future

After-Auction Buyer — Typically, a relative or close friend of the homeowner who could get a mortgage and buy the home after the auction, but who doesn't have the necessary cash to purchase the home at the auction

Internal Rate of Return — Abbreviated as IRR, is a measure of the profit earned by an investor on an investment. This measure is comparable to Return on Investment, ROI, Rate of Return, ROR, or Return. Return may be stated in dollars or a percentage.

Lease with Rider — The Lease is the contract between the landlord and tenant. The Rider in this strategy is made part of the Lease and includes the Purchase Option and other terms unique to the Foreclosure Friendly strategy.

ForeclosureFriendlies.com

Premier Foreclosure Friendly — Discussed and described more fully later, this is a Foreclosure Friendly with specific characteristics which make it more likely to be especially profitable to Investors

Chapter 1: A Brief History

Discovering Real Estate

Will Rogers often said, "We're all ignorant, only on different subjects." My subject was real estate. Even after graduating from college and later getting my MBA, I knew nothing about real estate. It wasn't taught at the schools I attended. I thought I had received a quality education in business, but I didn't know the first thing about real estate.

Then I read *How to Wake Up the Financial Genius Inside You* by Mark O. Haroldsen. It changed my life! Within the year, I read a dozen other real estate books, took the Illinois real estate licensing class, sat for the state exam, got my real estate Broker license, **and bought my first home (the first of several) with no money down. That was so, so easy! I'll explain how in the Postscript.** Then I quit my salaried day job and started a full-time real estate career.

A year or so after that, I started law school at night, while still working full-time and pursuing my real estate interests. Today I'm a licensed, practicing, real estate attorney with my own busy law firm. I'm also an instructor at my own real estate licensing school, and an active real estate investor. "Haroldsen on RE," as I call it, set me on a trajectory from which I've completed and helped others complete thousands of real estate transactions. The right book can do that for you. Thanks, Mark!

Flipping Foreclosures

In the year 2000, while working full-time as the Director of Global Real Estate for a large, multi-national corporation, I started dabbling in residential foreclosure properties. I bought my first foreclosure property at an auction in that year. Fortunately, it was vacant, so I didn't have to evict anyone. It was a small, two-bedroom condominium. My brother, Craig, helped me fix it up. In truth, Craig did most of the fixing up. He can fix or renovate anything in a home. You really need a Craig on your team if you're in the buying/renovating/flipping homes business. We sold that condominium in just a few months and made a tidy profit.

WHAT FUN! Thanks, Craig!

Pictured here is Craig. I highly recommend Investors incorporate a Craig or a similar model on their team!

Craig and I continued buying properties at foreclosure auctions while learning more about the process after that initial foreclosure success.

Foreclosure Investment Hits Close to Home

Shortly after I began buying foreclosure properties, I realized the substantial impact of taxes on the profit of the home sales. There was also a high holding cost while fixing up, marketing, and selling these homes. It was easy to see that significant savings would be available if we lived in the homes purchased at foreclosure auctions, fixed them up while living there, and sold them after one year to earn capital gains tax rates or after two years

Chapter 1: A Brief History

to have no taxes at all. That would generate significant additional profit with little or no taxes on any of the profit.

Instead of paying mortgage payments on my home during the year or more of renovating and marketing a foreclosure investment property, I could move into my foreclosure investment. I could then sell my current home and eliminate those mortgage payments. It would be a bit messy to remodel a foreclosure home while we lived there, but the savings would be spectacular, and it would be an exciting experience! So, let the adventure begin.

My family sold our third No Money Down home, described in the first Appendix and pictured on the front cover, and moved to Foreclosure Home #1. We remodeled that home while we lived there, sold it with a nice profit, and moved to Foreclosure Home #2. We renovated that home while we lived there, sold it later with a nice profit, and moved to Foreclosure Home #3. We renovated that home while we lived there, and that's where I live today, in Foreclosure Home #3.

If you're keeping score, we lived in four different homes in just five years. I got a low price on every home purchased at foreclosure auctions, and as a Managing Broker, I saved at least half of the real estate commission on every home sold. All the houses were located within a ten-mile radius, so we were able to stay close to family and friends. However, moving once is a pain, and no one wants to do it every couple of years. If you're young and single and have a strong back, go for it. Otherwise, there are other ways to make money in real estate, as is discussed in the following chapters.

As I was buying conventional auction properties to use as my residence, Craig and I continued to buy and flip larger and larger foreclosure auction properties until our last foreclosure flip in 2007... a home worth over $1,000,000. Unfortunately, the market was beginning its impending crash, and we barely made it out of that last flip with our shirts. That was the end of our conventional Foreclosure Flips, as we knew them back then.

The 2008 Foreclosure Crisis

In 2008, as the foreclosure crisis was getting underway, a Chicago Firm recruited me to develop a loan modification practice. I quickly developed financial analyses, spreadsheets, and a coordinated system. During that process, I learned how much I enjoyed helping distressed families save their homes. As a result, I opened a private law firm to handle loan modifications on my own.

The Rogers Law Group and the "Four Corner Defense"

A short time later, Margaret Cahill joined me. She was an experienced real estate attorney who had just turned down a position at that same Chicago Firm I had recently left. Thus, we officially became The Rogers Law Group, and she's still with me today, as of the writing of this book, heading up our Short Sale and Real Estate Closing transaction operations.

Regarding loan modifications, we soon learned that sometimes lenders just wouldn't do the right thing, and we had to say to them, "We'll see you in court." I looked for and found a good Foreclosure Defense litigator, George Olsen. He wasn't just good, he was exceptional! George was one of the co-authors of the Illinois Mortgage Foreclosure Law, and as I tell my clients, "There's no better attorney to have on your team than the man who wrote the law!"

Chapter 1: A Brief History

Over the first ten years of practice in the foreclosure arena, my tiny law firm grew to a team of 17 at its peak and helped more than 2,000 people save their homes through what we call "The Four Corner Defense: Foreclosure Defense, Mediation, Loan Modification, and Bankruptcy." We've also lectured and taught classes for hundreds of attorneys locally and across the nation on best practices in saving homes. It's been our crusade! I'm tremendously gratified by our successes for so many families in the Chicagoland area.

However, I've also tossed and turned through many sleepless nights over the years thinking about the family homes we couldn't save. Then in 2012, a client's home was sold at a foreclosure auction despite our best efforts to prevent it. Fortunately, after the auction, we were able to negotiate a deal for the homeowner and her family with the successful bidder at the auction.

Unwittingly, they became the first Friendly and Investor, and suddenly I had an "if all else fails" strategy – the Friendly Foreclosure strategy. The conclusion of that story is that this Friendly family repurchased their home from the Investor a few months after the auction for only a small fraction of what they owed on the house before the auction.

Red Lark and Beyond

There is too much risk and too little leverage for homeowners to wait and see if an investor will negotiate AFTER the foreclosure auction. We needed the investor to team up with the homeowner BEFORE the foreclosure auction. So, some friends and I got together and formed Red Lark, LLC, the first official Friendly Investor.

Not only was Red Lark able to keep foreclosed homeowners in their home when there were no other options left, but the Friendly Foreclosure strategy provided a strong return on investment for the Investors. We now had everything in place to really help Friendly Families as well as Investors.

Chapter 2: Conventional Foreclosures, Profits, & Lessons Learned

Before we get to the Friendly Foreclosure Strategy, it's important to understand the conventional foreclosure process. There are different foreclosure laws in different states, but for homeowners who don't pay their mortgage, eventually their home will likely be sold at a foreclosure auction, regardless of which state they call home. This book is not intended to be an instruction manual for the foreclosure process and you may have to decipher or adjust recommendations based on the different laws and procedures in your state.[1] The following segment is based on foreclosure auctions in Illinois.

Conventional Foreclosure Auctions

In this book, the term "conventional" refers to investors who don't know the homeowner, the investors typically won't have a ready tenant or buyer if they win the foreclosure auction, don't know the condition of the property other than what they can see from the street, and they're not permitted to tour the property prior to the auction. This is the typical scenario.

To give homeowners and investors an idea of the auction process, which will help you understand why the Friendly Foreclosure strategy came to be and how it is different, following is a description of how auctions work in the Chicagoland area:

---

[1] Do not rely on this book as legal advice. It is not! Sound legal advice will cost you far more than this book did. Please consult a local attorney before acting on any of the strategies described herein.

ForeclosureFriendlies.com

1. The foreclosing bank is required to advertise the auction 45 days before the scheduled date. The ad will typically include the address of the property, case number, location of the auction, and time and date advertised locally during the 45 days before the auction. From 10 to 50 properties may be auctioned off, consecutively, at a typical Chicago area auction.

2. Terms vary at auctions throughout the Chicago area. Auctions are open to the public, but auctioneers may choose to allow only bidders with cash or certified funds to attend the auction if there are space or other constraints at the location. Before the auction, attendants are often required to register and show their certified checks to the auctioneer. Some auctioneers will log in all registrants and the amount of funds they showed, thereby limiting the amount which they may bid at that auction. Auctioneers may also require investors to divulge the address of any properties on which they might bid.

3. Chicago area auctions typically require initial payments from the successful bidder in the amount of 10% or 25% of the total bid. Occasionally, an auctioneer will require 100% of the bid in certified funds at the auction.

4. At the appointed time or soon after, the auctioneer will begin by announcing a case name and number, the address of the relevant property, and the opening bid by the plaintiff. The auctioneer will not comment on the value of the property or disclose if the plaintiff is a first or second mortgage or judgment lien holder. Assume here, for example, the plaintiff, Bank of America, is the first mortgage lender, and has submitted an opening bid of $100,000. Assume also this home

Chapter 8: Finding Foreclosure Friendlies

has a Zillow estimated market value of $250,000. In this case, there are likely to be investors bidding.

5. The auctioneer will announce the opening bid of $100,000 by the plaintiff and will then ask, "Are there any other bids?" Foreclosure Auctions are Open-Cry, which means bidding is done out loud, as opposed to sealed bids. Attendants may raise their hands and announce their bid, which may start with as little as "a dollar over," which means one dollar over the opening bid, or in this case, $100,001.

   The next bid might be $101,000. Bids after that "dollar over" bid will typically go up by $1,000 or more, but sometimes less, based on desires by other bidders and the discretion of the auctioneer in the interest of time constraints. The bidding will continue until no bidder goes higher than the last bid.

6. That last and highest bidder will give the auctioneer the certified check, say $15,000 on a $150,000 successful bid if the auctioneer isn't already holding it. (Some auctioneers collect checks before the bidding starts.)

7. The winning bidder is required to pay the remaining balance due, in this case, $135,000, in certified funds or wire transfer within 24 or 48 hours, depending on that auctioneer's rules, or the bidder may lose the initial deposit. When the entire bid price is paid, the successful bidder receives a Certificate of Sale but does not yet own the property.

At some time after the auction date, typically at least two weeks to a month or two after the auction, a Motion to Approve the Sale will be scheduled for hearing at the Foreclosure Court. The motion is usually scheduled and presented by the Foreclosure Plaintiff. If the Sale is

Approved at that hearing, the winning bidder will receive a "Sheriff's Deed" soon thereafter. By Illinois Statute as of the writing of this book, the occupant of the home, usually the former owner, is allowed 30 days occupancy after the Sale is Confirmed. On day 31, the successful bidder/investor who is now the owner of the home, may have the Sheriff remove the occupants unless:

- At the Confirmation of Sale Hearing the judge gave the occupants more time to vacate, as judges occasionally do when asked, or
- The occupants are adults with a valid lease and are not named in the foreclosure case.

On the day the occupants are evicted, the new investor owners may remove all personal property from the premises and place it in the yard by the street for 24 hours for the former owners (or neighbors or anyone else) to pick through and take what they want. After 24 hours, the new owners may dispose of the remaining personal property that was placed by the street. As you can imagine, that's an ugly scenario.

Foreclosure Auction Lessons Learned:

"If that damn bank is going to take my home, it's not going to be in great shape when they get it!" When people spend months, and sometimes years in their home, not knowing if or when the bank will take it away, they don't maintain it as they otherwise would. As of 2018, foreclosures in Illinois typically take about a year and a half to complete after the homeowners miss their first mortgage payment. You can imagine the amount of disrepair that can happen in that timeframe. Some of the foreclosure auction homes we purchased were atrocious. At best, they were neglected for a year or longer. At worst, the distressed homeowners took

Chapter 8: Finding Foreclosure Friendlies

out their financial frustrations on their homes, sometimes trashing them before leaving. One house we bought had been stripped of every appliance, light fixture, interior door—even the lightbulbs were gone! Right or wrong, this is the prevalent mindset of many homeowners in foreclosure, particularly when the bank won't negotiate reasonably for a loan modification or other loss mitigation solution. Whether the damage is extreme or normal wear and tear, it will often take months to remove the occupants and then clean, repair, renovate, and put the property on the market for rent or sale. (Add another few months, depending on the time of year, to sell at a reasonable price and to close on the deal. In all, the time from winning the auction to renting or selling the home typically took us 6–12 months.)

Possession & Unknown Occupants. After winning at a foreclosure auction in Illinois, obtaining possession of the property free of occupants will typically take 3–6 months. It could take much longer if there is a valid lease. The sheriff can go to the house to evict the former owners after the auction, but if tenants are living there, the sheriff will not evict anyone. The sheriff will report back to the new owner, who will often have to file a lawsuit to rid the home of the tenants which can take an extra 90 days or more to gain possession of the property. If the tenant has a valid lease, the new owner will usually have to honor that lease.

First in Time, First in Right. A clear understanding of the condition of title is essential. While this may vary from state to state, one can't assume that all liens, other mortgages, homeowner association liens, mechanics liens, unpaid taxes, and judgments will be removed from the title when the Sheriff's Deed is issued after the auction. If investors make mistakes in this area, those mistakes could easily cost tens of thousands, or even hundreds of thousands, of dollars.

Estimating Profits on Conventional Foreclosure Auctions

When buying at a foreclosure auction, investors will usually not get to see the property in advance of the auction. Therefore, it's an inexact process to generate a reasonable estimate of market value in good, finished condition, and then deduct the estimated cost to put it in that condition. This is important for homeowners to know, so they can understand an investor's perspective and what parameters they follow.

Following is what Craig and I did when we were buying foreclosure properties at the auction to flip:

Step 1: Estimate the "finished fair market value" of the home. Most of the time, the home was not listed for sale, and we didn't have access to inspect the house before the auction, so this was not an easy task. However, we were able to compare homes of similar sizes and amenities (often called "comparables" or "comps") and sometimes research prior listings for the property in question.

> *If you're regularly bidding or planning to do so at foreclosure auctions, it's a good idea to have a licensed real estate broker on your team or to otherwise have access to your local MLS. If you're actively buying and selling foreclosure properties, you need that MLS!*

Throughout this book, especially when referring to auction bidding, I'll mention the essential factor of market value. Please note I am referring to "finished fair market value" which means the market value of that home in reasonably good condition. Typically, homes going to auction will not be

Chapter 8: Finding Foreclosure Friendlies

in good shape, and so a cost to put them in such condition is built into an investor's bid calculations unless it is a Friendly Foreclosure purchase.

Step 2: Estimate the cost of clean-up, general repairs, and renovation. We used 10% of the finished fair market value as our estimate. That's possible for investors with a Craig on their team, a partner who does a lot of the work with no labor charge in return for a split of the profits. If investors don't have a Craig, their renovation costs may average closer to 20% or above. Only experience will give a good handle on that crucial estimate because investors won't see most of the homes before the auction. Investors won't be able to see the work that must be done or gather bids on that work before the auction.

Step 3: Estimate the closing costs. As a licensed real estate broker, I would list the property myself, saving half of the real estate commission. To get the best price, investors must list the home in the MLS. We did so, and paid buyer brokers a 2.5% commission. In Illinois, investors will also have to pay real estate tax prorations, title, and closing costs, attorney fees, transfer taxes, survey costs, and other closing costs. As an attorney and title agent and real estate broker, my closing costs were substantially lower than most. Our closing costs still amounted to 6-8% of the sale price. That's a big part of the profit.

> 💰 *Avoiding commissions and reducing closing costs will be a considerable advantage to profit margins. So, if you can get an attorney or real estate broker on your investment team, that will save you thousands on every transaction.*

Between the foreclosure auction and the subsequent sale closing date, investor costs in Illinois, as a percentage of Market Value may be:

10-20%   Renovation and Holding Costs after Auction

10%   Closing Costs for Resale

20-30%   Total Costs… call it 25%

If an investor's estimated total cost of the project is 25% of the home's finished fair market value, then the break-even auction bid price is 75% of the estimated finished fair market value. Investors don't buy high-risk properties, sight unseen, at foreclosure auctions with a plan to break even. Investing is their job, so they are looking to make money on the deal. They should build in a minimum estimated profit of 10% of the final sale price. That means investors must buy properties at foreclosure auctions for a maximum price of 65% of the estimated finished resale price.

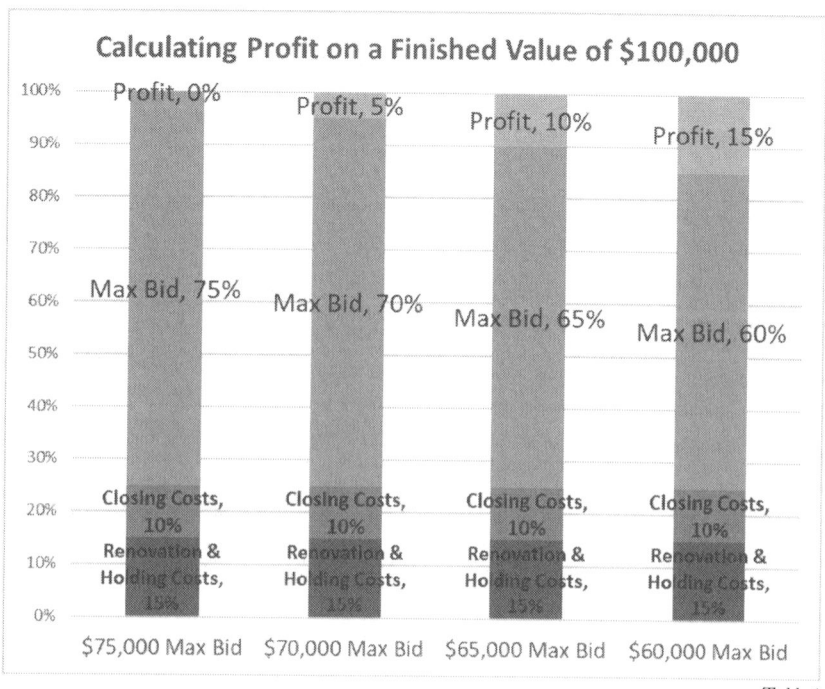

Table 1

Chapter 8: Finding Foreclosure Friendlies

Most experienced foreclosure property investors, or "regulars," know this. Regulars rarely bid more than 65% of finished fair market value. They scowl and swear under their breath at rookies who bid too high at foreclosure auctions. However, as discussed in Chapter 6, "Determining and Negotiating Terms," Friendly Foreclosure Investors can bid 70-80% of the estimated market value and still make spectacular profits!

In summary, it's important for you as a homeowner to know what investors are up against when they look to buy a foreclosure home. That's why I believe the Foreclosure Friendly strategy is so important! It offers different options than a conventional auction can provide to investors, making your foreclosure property more attractive to them. An added benefit for investors is that they go into it knowing that they are helping someone in the process.

When homeowners' homes are at stake, they can feel their world crumbling. That's understandable on every level. By and large, these are good people who are trying their best to meet their obligations. Life may have just dealt them a bad hand. As an investor, you have the chance to do a great deed for them. A definite win-win opportunity for both sides!

Chapter 3: Foreclosure Friendlies in a Nutshell

Conventional Foreclosure Investment v. the Friendly Foreclosure

When a property is sold at a conventional foreclosure auction, investors bid sight unseen, with hopes to buy it at a significant discount. The winning investor will be the new owner of a property, likely occupied by a family who doesn't want to leave, is very upset about losing their home, and has no obligation to maintain the property or pay rent while they continue to live there. The investor faces the ugly task of evicting the family, and the family faces the ugly task of packing up and getting out.

A Friendly Foreclosure is different—the investor and the homeowner are on the same team. They're friendly! Together they receive a mutually beneficial outcome:

The Friendly Homeowners, or **Friendlies**, get to stay in their home after the auction at an affordable monthly rent, with the option to purchase their home back in the future for less than what they owed to their mortgage lender before the foreclosure auction.

The Friendly Investor, or **Investor**, buys a cash flow positive property, at a significant discount, avoids the eviction process and expenses for repairs, maintenance, and marketing for resale, and ends up with a greater Return on Investment "ROI" in the end!

Foreclosure Flips provide exceptional profits. Foreclosure *Holds* offer a longer-term wealth building program with an immediate net worth boost.

ForeclosureFriendlies.com

The Friendly Foreclosure Process[2]

At the Friendly Foreclosure auction, the Investor will bid and hopefully win. If successful, the Friendly will become a tenant and lease the home from the Investor under a pre-agreed, affordable rental lease. The Lease will usually be one to three years and will include a Purchase Option, whereby the Friendlies may purchase the property back at any time during the lease term at a pre-arranged price based on the finished market value. That Purchase Option price will be significantly less than the amount the Friendly previously owed on the home and more than the investor bid at the auction. The rent will typically be less than the former mortgage payment which provides savings to the Friendly while covering costs and providing some immediate revenue for the Investor.

The Friendly and the Investor sign the Lease and Purchase Option before the auction. However, there should be <u>no deposits or any exchange of money</u> between Friendly and Investor before the auction. **The Friendly should NOT pay any money to the Investor before the auction!**

If the Investor is the successful bidder, the lease both parties already signed will be in effect the day after the auction. If the Investor loses at the auction, the Lease and Purchase Option will be null and void, and the Friendly and the Investor will be financially no better or worse off than if they had done nothing. So, winning can be spectacular, and losing would be "as if you did nothing at all." Not much of a gamble.

---

[2] Note that all suggestions in this book are subject to the laws of your state and local jurisdiction. You may want to contact a local attorney for that discussion, as nothing in this book is deemed legal or tax advice. For example, some municipalities have specific lease requirements regarding security deposits. Be sure to investigate any lease regulations in your area before signing one.

Chapter 8: Finding Foreclosure Friendlies

This strategy changes the foreclosure auction from a final nail in the foreclosure coffin to an opportunity for financial redemption for the homeowner.

 The Friendly Foreclosure strategy is successful because the Friendly is not just any homeowner in foreclosure, but specifically, a formerly financially distressed, now a fully or partially financially recovered homeowner in foreclosure. Friendlies have a strong desire to keep their home and the financial capability to do so but have exhausted all other possible avenues of escape from foreclosure. As an Investor, you really do have the power to give families an escape from foreclosure and the optimal solution to the devastating loss of their home. That's a miracle to them!

A Friendly Foreclosure in its Simplest Form

An Illinois woman bought her home in 2006, at the height of the market, for $300,000. In 2007, she lost her job. By 2009, she had been rejected three times for loan modification applications, the mortgage was 12 months behind, and the lender had filed a foreclosure case against her.

By 2010:

- Including attorney fees and court costs added to her mortgage, past due payments, late fees, and penalties, she then owed $350,000 on her mortgage. With the market crash, her home was now worth $200,000.
- After six months of unemployment, she was working again but didn't have the funds necessary to reinstate her mortgage.

- Because the lender had a history of bidding 75% of market value, or less, at foreclosure auctions, there was a good chance this property could be purchased for $150,000 or less at the auction.

With a Friendly Foreclosure strategy:

- A Friendly Investor was identified and purchased the home for $150,000 at the auction.
- The former owner, or Friendly, leased the home from the Investor for one year at a rent lower than her prior mortgage payment, but which provided a 10% ROI to the investor.
- One year after the auction, the Friendly repurchased her home from the Investor for $200,000. After a down-payment of $6,000, she owed $194,000 on her new, affordable mortgage rather than the $350,000 she owed before the home was sold at a foreclosure auction.
- The repurchase provided $50,000 of gross profit upon sale to the Investor, a 33% ROI in addition to the 10% rent return for the Investor. Not too shabby!
- The foreclosing lender also made out nicely here, as it recovered $150,000 from the auction. Generally, the foreclosing lender recovers less than 50% of the fair market value, which would be less than $100,000 in this case, and on average it takes lenders a year after the auction to do so.

The above is a common story about how people end up in foreclosure, with homes that are "upside down" or "underwater," meaning they owe more than the home is worth. The Foreclosure Friendly strategy is designed to assist Friendlies with similar circumstances.

Chapter 8: Finding Foreclosure Friendlies

The following chapters will explain the steps of this strategy in greater detail – but first a few frequently asked questions:

Will I need an attorney during my foreclosure process if I go with the Foreclosure Friendly strategy?

 Yes. This book describes a real estate transaction. Buying or selling a home is the largest financial transaction you will likely complete in your life. The Foreclosure Friendly transaction is not particularly complicated, but it is a bit different than conventional real estate transactions. Therefore, find an attorney to assist you. It's not essential, but it's a good idea to have an attorney represent you from the start.

Your attorney should review the lease and rider offered by the Investor. That will take an attorney only a short time and shouldn't cost much. However, those documents are vitally important. Later, when you exercise the Purchase Option, you should also have an attorney represent you. That representation will be similar to a conventional real estate purchase closing. Any experienced real estate closing attorney can handle the initial document review and the closing when you exercise your Purchase Option. If you're in the Chicago area, feel free to call my office to inquire about legal representation.

Will I need an attorney during the Investment process of buying a foreclosed home if I go with the Foreclosure Friendly strategy?

Yes. It's a good idea. Particularly important is the condition of title. An attorney will best be able to help you sort that out. It can be incredibly costly if you get that wrong.

This Foreclosure Friendly strategy sounds great, but is it all legal?

Absolutely! It's interesting to me that this is a common question I am asked about the Friendly Foreclosure strategy. That's probably because there are other real estate transactions that don't allow what the Friendly Foreclosure strategy allows. For example, with short sales, buyers are typically prohibited by the seller's mortgage servicer from renting or selling the property back to the former owner. That's the right of the mortgage servicer, not the law. Many assume the same is true for foreclosure auctions.

In Illinois, it is not illegal for Investors at foreclosure auctions to rent or sell the property back to the former owner. In fact, anyone, including the former owner, may bid at a foreclosure auction in Illinois, notwithstanding their plans for the home after the auction. To do otherwise, in my opinion, would be an unreasonable restraint of trade and would have an unfair and improper negative impact on the homeowner. Also, the more bidders, the higher the auction sale price is likely to be, which is good for the mortgage servicers. These servicers want as high of an amount paid as possible at the foreclosure auctions, and they aren't overly concerned about the source of the bid.

If you're at all worried about the legality of this strategy in your state, consult a local attorney competent in foreclosure matters. If that attorney says it would not be legal, consult a different attorney. I don't believe it is illegal anywhere, and I would like to know if you are told differently by any competent attorney active in the foreclosure practice area.

To my knowledge, this practice is not unlawful anywhere at the time of this writing. There may be some attorneys who don't understand the

Chapter 8: Finding Foreclosure Friendlies

Foreclosure Friendly strategy, or they confuse auction buying with short sale buying. I would be happy to talk to them to clear up any confusion.

The benefits of this strategy are significant for the homeowner in foreclosure, the Investor buying at the auction, and even the bank that is foreclosing. I've seen it work and when it does, all parties are usually elated with the results. After all, that's why I do this!

Chapter 4: Foreclosure Friendly Flips and Holds

Real estate investors may be classified as either holders or flippers. Holders want to keep the investment property and collect rent over a long-term as the property appreciates in value and the mortgage decreases. Flippers want to buy and sell property quickly, capture the profit as soon as possible, and move on to the next deal. The Friendly Foreclosure program is designed more for holders, but as you'll see, it can work very nicely for flippers, too. Following are a few examples of both.

Example #1 – A Friendly Foreclosure Flip

The Friendly

Dad lost his job and was unemployed for an extended period. The home fell into foreclosure. Dad got a great, new job, but didn't have the tens of thousands of dollars required to catch up on the mortgage, as well as the utility bills, credit card bills, and other overdue bills. The bank refused to work with Dad to modify his mortgage and instead continued the foreclosure.

Dad and his family of four were desperate to keep the home. It appraised at $205,000, but with all the arrearage and real estate taxes and fees, they owed well over $400,000 on the home. They couldn't sell it, couldn't refinance, and even if the bank agreed to modify their mortgage payments (which they wouldn't) it would be years, if ever, before they would ever have equity in the home again.

Grandma, who also lived in the home, had excellent credit and qualified for her own FHA mortgage to buy the house at the current market value, but the bank wouldn't consider an offer by Grandma to buy the home as a short sale, because she was a related party and wanted to lease it and later sell it back to the original owners, her son and his family. While that is the case for short sale transactions, no such restriction exists for auction purchases, but unfortunately, Grandma didn't have the required cash to bid at the auction.

So, with the knowledge that Grandma could be the After-Auction Buyer with a mortgage, we looked for and found an Investor to buy the property at the auction and then sell it back to Grandma. The After-Auction Buyer, Grandma, made this an attractive opportunity for an Investor who was looking to flip a property.

The Investor

This purchase would be the first Friendly Foreclosure for this Investor, a couple who had previous real estate investment experience. They secured the money to invest from their self-directed IRA. It was a bit cumbersome, but it worked.

They met with the Friendly and his family, reviewed their financials to confirm they could afford the short-term rent, and then inspected the home. They obtained a copy of the pre-qualification letter from Grandma's mortgage company, and though not typical of most Investors, they paid for a formal appraisal of the home. The home appraised for a market value of $205,000, and the Investors were willing to bid up to $164,000 or 80% of

Chapter 8: Finding Foreclosure Friendlies

market value. The Investors and Friendlies signed a Lease with a Purchase Option, contingent upon the Investor winning the auction.

Next came the auction. The bank opened the bidding with $157,349, which was about 77% of the estimated fair market value. The Friendly Investor bid $1 over the opening bid. The auctioneer asked for any other bids, and the room was silent.

"Going once, going twice...sold!" to the Friendly Investor! Conventional investors will typically not bid that high a percentage of estimated fair market value, because that auction price would leave no profit for the investor. So, it makes sense that in this case, the Friendly Investor had no competition and won the bid for $157,350.

The Friendly family rented the home from the Investor for less than three months after the auction, until the court confirmed the auction sale and Grandma got her mortgage to buy back the house from the Investor. Grandma incurred some mortgage application costs, a small down payment on the FHA mortgage, closing costs, and attorney fees for the re-purchase which of course, the Friendly family reimbursed to her.

The FHA assumable mortgage is an attractive aspect of this Friendly Foreclosure outcome because it means when the Friendly's credit and mortgage eligibility permit, the Friendly can purchase the home and assume Grandma's low interest, fixed rate loan, with no down payment and little to no change in the terms. All Friendlies should be vigilant for a similar opportunity with an FHA, VA, or other assumable mortgage loan from an After-Auction Buyer.

ForeclosureFriendlies.com

The Friendly's "Before and After" Financial Summaries:

	Before the Auction	2 ½ Mo. Rental Period	After the Re-purchase
Total Owed on the Home	$460,000	N/A	$199,875
Monthly House Payments	$3,083	$2,000	$1,793

Note that the total Principal Balance due on the home, and the monthly payments, were both drastically reduced for the Friendlies. That, and saving the home, are the goals of Foreclosure Friendly transactions.

The Investor's Financial Summary:

Investor Winning Bid at the Auction	$157,350
Sale Price to Grandma 2½ Months Later	$205,000
Profit over 2 ½ months	$ 47,650
Return on Investment	30%

The 2½ months of rent received by the Investors exceeded their cost of completing this transaction. Therefore, the exact profits were slightly higher than that calculated above. That's not too bad for the Investors' first Friendly Foreclosure! Moreover, after making a 30% Return on that Investment, they still had 9½ months left in the year to reinvest their proceeds in other Friendly Foreclosure opportunities or elsewhere.

Chapter 8: Finding Foreclosure Friendlies
Example #2 – Another Friendly Foreclosure Flip

The Friendly

This family had been fighting for years to keep their home. They had been through numerous applications for a loan modification, a long foreclosure case, and a bankruptcy. Now the end was drawing near, the auction was coming soon, and they had run out of options.

Their attorney sent them to me to see if I could help them with my Friendly Foreclosure strategy. Although they were facing a foreclosure auction, their finances were otherwise in good shape. They had recovered from their previous financial difficulties, and with their current income, they could afford to keep their home. To make matters even better, they had an FHA mortgage, which meant the bank would probably bid low at the Auction.

It's worth noting that they were about the nicest family you could ever meet. After visiting with them and inspecting their home, one of my partners, Chris, reported, "Rick, we have to help this family! They are exactly the type of people we formed our group to help! We have to help them!" OK, Chris. We'll try!

ForeclosureFriendlies.com

The Investor

This opportunity arose soon after I obtained my LIRP[3], and I was anxious to put it to the test. This auction would be my first Friendly Foreclosure purchase funded with my LIRP.

After confirming the sound financial condition of the Friendlies, and inspecting the home, we estimated the finished market value to be $307,500 and agreed to move forward. Since this was a Premier Foreclosure Friendly, we determined we could bid up to 80% of the market value and still be confident of making a stellar profit.

Then we learned that her dad wanted to help but didn't have the available cash to bid at the auction. He didn't live far away, and he had the necessary credit score, so we directed him to a good mortgage broker, who pre-qualified him to buy the home for $307,500. Dad would now be our After-Auction Buyer. That made this an excellent flip opportunity.

We signed a Lease with an assignable Purchase Option with the Friendlies, contingent upon our winning the auction. Then we went to the auction.

We expected the opening bid to be low because it was an FHA mortgage. Surprise! It was not a low bid. The bank bid $229,951, which was almost 75% of the market value. Fortunately, we were prepared to bid high if necessary. We bid "$1 over" the opening bid, and no other investors

---

[3] Life Insurance Retirement Plan – see Chapter 10.

had any interest at that high auction price, so, we won the property for $229,952!

The Friendly's "Before and After" financial summaries:

	Before the Auction	2 ½ Mo. Rental Period	After the Re-purchase
Total Owed on the Home	$465,000	N/A	$307,500
Monthly House Payment	$3,494	$2,500	$2,354

Note that the amount due on the home and the monthly payments were reduced dramatically in both aforementioned Foreclosure Friendly transactions, as is the goal for all such transactions.

The Investor's Financial Summary:

Winning Bid at the Auction	$229,952
Sale Price to Dad 2 ½ Months Later	$307,500
Profit over 2 ½ Months	$77,548
Return on Investment	34%

In this transaction, the rent for 2 ½ months more than covered the transaction costs. Therefore, the Return on Investment was 34% in just 2 ½ months! As you can see, these Friendly Foreclosures can work nicely for flippers.

If we did projects like this back to back all year, the annual profit would amount to 162%, which would more than double our money. If you have sufficient cash resources, you don't have to do the projects back to back.

You can do them side by side, not waiting to finish one before starting the next, and thereby increasing your profits.

Now you've seen how to do a Friendly Foreclosure flip while helping a nice family and making a spectacular profit. I've been a flipper at heart for my entire real estate career. However, in recent years I've been leaning more and more toward becoming a holder. My partners and I have paid some ugly ordinary income taxes on spectacular flip profits. Had we held the home for a year or more or done a tax-free exchange for a property we would hold, we could have qualified for Long-Term Capital Gains tax treatment on our profit, thereby cutting our taxes almost in half or deferring them entirely for many years. That's certainly something worth considering.

Regarding the flips described above, the Friendlies made out great, as did the Investors. Even the foreclosing banks[4] had impressive results!

Now that we've had some fun playing with Foreclosure Friendly flips, we'll next learn how Friendly Foreclosures more often work, as medium-term holds.

---

[4] Banks are lucky to recover 50% of the market value of a home after foreclosure, and on average it takes them about a year after the auction to do so. In these cases, using this strategy, the banks got 75% and 77% of the market value. That's about 50% more than they usually recover, and they did it in a month instead of a year. Those are spectacular results for the banks! See Postscript III for more details.

Chapter 8: Finding Foreclosure Friendlies

Example #3 – A Friendly Foreclosure Hold

The Friendly

Following is a more typical example of a Friendly Foreclosure transaction:

A mom had recently gone through a divorce, which is a frequent theme among those in foreclosure. She and her two sons, a freshman and junior in high school, were facing a foreclosure auction in just 30 days.

She had recently completed a Chapter 7 Bankruptcy and had no debt. She was working full-time, and after the bankruptcy could afford the home. However, she didn't have the $45,000 necessary to reinstate the mortgage and stop the auction.

Because of the impact of the foreclosure and bankruptcy on her credit, she wasn't confident she would be able to find or qualify to rent another affordable home in the school district if she lost this home. Although it didn't make much sense to try and save a home worth $300,000, for which she owed over $400,000, she was desperate to stay in the house because her two children had lived there all their lives and had been through more than enough trauma with the divorce.

The Friendly homeowner had no family or close friends with the financial capability of buying the home at or even after the auction.

ForeclosureFriendlies.com

The Investor

The Investor we identified owned a two-flat apartment building nearby but had never bought a Friendly Foreclosure property. The Investor inspected the Friendly's home and reviewed her pay stubs, checking account statements, child support provision of the marital settlement agreement, most recent mortgage statement, and prior year's tax return. The Investor determined the Friendly had a steady and secure job as a nurse, with stable income, reasonable expenses, a ten-year-old home in excellent condition, and a Fannie Mae loan. The Investor and Friendly got along well and decided to move forward with each other and to discuss the terms of a Friendly Foreclosure Lease agreement.

The Investor agreed to bid up to $225,000 at the auction. That's 75% of the $300,000 estimated market value. Since the home had a Fannie Mae loan, there was a good chance the Investor would win that auction. Before the auction, the Investor and Friendly signed a 36-month Lease with a Purchase Option. The Lease was clear that no money would change hands until and unless the Investor was the successful bidder at the auction.

At the auction the bank's opening bid was $220,000, roughly 73% of the estimated market value. Once again, there was no competition for the Friendly Investor as conventional investors would have had little or no profit, and possibly a loss, if they bid over 73%.

The lease went into effect immediately after the Auction. A quick summary of the terms:

Chapter 8: Finding Foreclosure Friendlies

Rent based on 8% ROI + Taxes & Insurance (increases 5% each year)		Purchase Option Price (increases 3% each year)	
$1,800	Monthly Gross Rent in Year 1	$300,000	Purchase Option Price in Year 1
$1,875	Monthly Gross Rent in Year 2	$309,000	Purchase Option Price in Year 2
$1,954	Monthly Gross Rent in Year 3	$318,270	Purchase Option Price in Year 3

Rent, based on an 8% return on the maximum bid by the Investor, plus $300 reimbursement for real estate tax and insurance costs, totaled $1,800 per month. The Purchase Option Price, $300,000, would increase 3% each year, eventually reaching $318,270 after the third anniversary of the Lease.

The Friendly's "Before and Projected After" Financial Summaries:

	Before the Auction	36 Month Rental Period	After the Re-Purchase
Total Owed on the Home	$428,000	N/A	$318,270
Monthly House Payments	$2,300	$1,800 + 5% yearly escalations	$1,949

Note the savings for the Friendly: Rent was initially about $500 per month less than her prior mortgage payments, and although it would increase annually, the savings would allow her to save up a down-payment over the next three years. Additionally, when she was able to get a mortgage three years later, she was able to repurchase the home for over $100,000 less than what she owed on her mortgage before the auction.

The Friendly Foreclosure Strategy changed this Friendly's life. Not only was she able to keep her home when all seemed lost, but her monthly payments were reduced, and she had a chance once again to build equity in her home. Her two sons were able to graduate high school in the same school district in which they've always attended. It was a spectacular result for the Friendly and her family.

The Investor's Financial Summary:

Now let's see how the Investor made out using the Friendly Foreclosure Strategy:

	Pre-Tax Analysis of a Three-Year Hold
($220,001)	Initial Investment/Winning Auction Bid
$67,548	Gross rent over 3 years (5% increase/year)
($10,800)	less Taxes & Insurance (roughly $300/mo.)
$318,270	Purchase Option Price in Year 3 (3% increase/year)
($25,462)	less Closing Costs (8%)
$129,555	Profit over 3 years

In the above transaction, the Investor had a $129,555 return over three years which is an annual Internal Rate of Return[5] of 19%. That's a good rate of return for any year, and even better when it's the average return over multiple years, as it is above. Let's compare the hold to the same scenario

---

[5] An internal rate of return is a complex financial calculation used to analyze and compare the profitability of investment options. It is especially helpful when evaluating the future returns of different real estate projects.

Chapter 8: Finding Foreclosure Friendlies

if the Investor had been able to flip the property to an After-Auction Buyer.

Pre-Tax Analysis of a 3-Year Hold		Pre-Tax Flip to After-Auction Buyer	
($220,001)	Winning Auction Bid	($220,001)	Winning Auction Bid
$67,548	Gross rent over 3 years	$4,500	Gross Rent over 2 ½ Months
($10,800)	less Taxes & Insurance	($750)	less Taxes & Insurance
$318,270	Purchase Option Price in Year 3	$300,000	Purchase Option Price after 2 ½ Mo.
($25,462)	less Closing Costs (8%)	($6,000)	less Closing Costs (2%)
$129,555	Profit over 3 years	$77,749	Profit after 2 ½ months
19%	Annual Internal Rate of Return	353% [6]	Annual Internal Rate of Return

Table 2

Friendly Foreclosure Holds do not produce the spectacularly quick returns Friendly Foreclosure Flips often do. However, the holds generally offer higher total cash returns and lower income taxes over extended periods. If this were the only deal the Investor ever did – the hold would result in a greater cash return ($129,555), but it would take 33 months longer than the flip. On the other hand, the flip would give more ambitious Investors the opportunity to reinvest their funds and potentially make a

---

[6] Note that quick returns can provide an outrageously high and misleading Annual Internal Rate of Return like the 353% return shown above.

$70,000+ return fourteen more times in that same three years. As you can see, there are considerable benefits to holders, as well as flippers, using the Friendly Foreclosure Strategy.

Double Your Returns on Foreclosure Friendly Holds!

In the previous example, the Investor achieved a 19% Rate of Return on the hold investment. The Investor paid 73% of the market value at the auction and received rent based on an 8% yearly return of the maximum auction bid. Compared to a conventional investor who would have to evict the current tenant, repair the property, find a renter and hope to sell – the Friendly Investor's results are spectacular! But in Friendly Foreclosure terms these results are average, not remarkable. The quality of the Friendly and the home may have made that transaction above average, but the financial conditions and profit were not exceptional for a Friendly Foreclosure and would have been far better if the homeowner had been a Premier Foreclosure Friendly.

You can double the Rate of Return by using a mortgage. Let's look at this same transaction with a mortgage. Note that one can't use a mortgage contingency when bidding at an auction, so you'll still have to come up with the cash or use a line of credit for the auction, but you can apply for a mortgage right after the auction.

Assume the Investor paid cash at the auction, and then applied for a mortgage with the following terms:

Chapter 8: Finding Foreclosure Friendlies

75% of Auction Price is the Mortgage Loan Amount
5% Interest-Only Monthly Payments
1% Origination Fee
$500 in other fees

Note the mortgage terms above are those available as of the writing of this book. An Investor's mortgage terms will undoubtedly vary and will impact their Internal Rate of Return. When doing the math, Investors will be happy to learn a higher mortgage rate will not have a dramatic effect on their Rate of Return.

Consider the following terms of a Three-Year Hold with a Mortgage

$220,001	Initial Investment/Winning Auction Bid
$2,700	Initial Rent on day 1 after the Auction (pro-rated rent + 1 month advance rent)
$1,800	Monthly gross rent in Year 1 (8% rent rate + $300 taxes & insurance)
$1,875	Monthly gross rent in Year 2 (8% rent rate + $300 taxes & insurance + 5% increase/year)
$1,954	Monthly gross rent in Year 3 (8% rent rate + $300 taxes & insurance + 5% increase/year)
$165,001	75% LTV Mortgage
$162,251	Mortgage payout to Investor (after $500 App + 1% costs + Taxes & Insurance Escrow)
$988	Monthly Mortgage Payment (5% Interest Only + $300 taxes & insurance)
$812	Net rent after mortgage, taxes & insurance
$318,270	Purchase Option Price in Year 3 (escalated 3%/year)
8%	Re-Sale Closing Costs
$292,808	Net Proceeds of the Re-Sale

Table 3

The Internal Rate of Return, demonstrated in Table 4, increases from 19% to 45% by using a mortgage. The reason is that although the cash return (or profit) is impacted relatively slightly, the investment is cut by almost 75% under the mortgage terms illustrated.

Pre-Tax Comparison of Three-Year Hold with and Without a Mortgage

Month			Without a Mortgage	With a Mortgage
0	01/15/14	Auction bid less initial prorated rent	($217,301)	($217,301)
1	02/01/14	Net Rent	$1,500	$1,500
2	03/01/14	Net Rent + cash mortgage payout	$1,500	**$164,051**
3	04/01/14	Net Rent	$1,500	$812
...	Months 4 - 11			
12	01/01/15	Net Rent	$1,500	$812
13	02/01/15	**Net Rent increased 3%**	**$1,575**	**$902**
14	03/01/15	Net Rent	$1,575	$902
...	Months 15-24			
24	01/01/16	Net Rent	$1,575	$902
25	02/01/16	**Net Rent increased 3%**	**$1,654**	**$997**
26	03/01/16	Net Rent	$1,654	$997
...	Months 27-35			
36	01/01/17	Net Rent	$1,654	$997
37	02/01/17	**Profit upon resale**	**$292,808**	**$128,757**
		Return on Investment	$129,555	$105,339
Annual Internal Rate of Return			**19%**	**45%**

Table 4

Chapter 8: Finding Foreclosure Friendlies

Get better mortgage terms, and you'll get even better rates of return. You'll have to agree—a 45% average annual return is not bad. With that rate of return, you can double your money in less than two years. If you can get a mortgage quicker or use a line of credit to purchase at the auction, rather than using your own cash, your Internal Rate of Return will be even higher.

Leverage

The increased Internal Rate of Return shown in Table 4 is brought about by leverage. For illustration purposes, the following is a simple example of leverage:

- If an Investor bought a property for $100,000 cash and sold it a year later with a $10,000 net profit, the Investor made a 10% return on the investment.

- If an Investor bought that same property for the same price of $100,000 using a mortgage with a 10% down payment of $10,000 and sold it a year later after net mortgage and expense costs of $5,000, the profit would only be $5,000. However, the initial investment was only $10,000. So, the return would be $5,000 on a $10,000 investment or a 50% return.

The 50% Rate of Return on the property transaction in the example above is five times higher with a mortgage than without one! Purchase and sale price of the property and all expenses are the same. The only difference is the use of a mortgage. That difference quintuples the return on investment. That increase in the Return is due to leverage.

You may have heard negative feedback about leverage. It can make investors wealthy, and it can also tumble a financial empire. It can multiply earnings in times of escalating values of real estate and the stock market. However, leverage has decimated many highly leveraged investors during downturns of the economy. Investors should be aware of the principle and use it when it makes sense. Leverage should provide increased profit with manageable risk.

For the mortgage on the Friendly Foreclosure described at the beginning of this chapter, the Investor would be borrowing 75% of the winning bid. That winning bid was about 74% of the market value of the property.

So, the mortgage loan would be 75% of 74% of the market value of the home.

That equates to a mortgage of $165,000 on a $300,000 home, which is only 56% of the property value. That's a conservative loan with low risk on a single-family, pre-leased, rental home investment.

You also have a long-term tenant who is devoted to staying in the property and who wants to buy it at a significant profit to you, and who will pay you a handsome rent until able to do so. You must judge the risk of all your investments yourself.

I don't perceive the addition of a 56% Loan-to-Value mortgage as an unreasonable risk at all for this type of transaction. Given that it would more than double the annual return, I wouldn't think twice about taking that mortgage. In addition to doubling my Rate of Return, it would provide me a refund of nearly 75% of my investment capital to invest in other Friendly Foreclosures or elsewhere.

Chapter 8: Finding Foreclosure Friendlies

In summary, Friendly Foreclosures can be quick flips or they can be short, medium, or long term holds. Regardless of their timing aspects, Friendly Foreclosures can provide dramatic profits to the Investors. Use some leverage with a mortgage or line of credit, and Investors may double their already attractive returns. This impressive profit is on top of the personal satisfaction of saving the homes of deserving families who are at the center of the Friendly Foreclosure strategy.

Chapter 5: Qualifications of a Good Foreclosure Friendly Candidate

Are You a Premier Foreclosure Friendly?

This chapter discusses the aspects of a Foreclosure Friendly candidate which make it attractive to an Investor. The chapter goes further to define a "Premier Foreclosure Friendly."

 If you're in foreclosure and want to keep your home, you need to know what will make your situation most appealing to an Investor. You also want to determine if you are a Premier Foreclosure Friendly, which means your home has a higher likelihood of success and maximum profits. That will naturally draw considerable attention from Investors.

 If you're an Investor, this will provide a helpful guide in the evaluation of the quality of the Foreclosure Friendly you're considering.

Following is a list of Foreclosure Friendly qualifications:

1. ***Underwater/Upside Down Home.*** The value of the home <u>must</u> be less than the total balance due on all mortgages and liens. Being underwater is a prerequisite. The whole premise of a Friendly Foreclosure is that the Friendly will have the option to purchase their home from the Investor after the auction at market value. If the homeowner already owes less than market value–that's not a good deal. If homeowners have equity, they should make every effort to sell the home and collect the equity before the foreclosure sale.

2. ***Desire to Keep the Home.*** The second most important qualification of a Friendly is the desire to keep the home. The reasons can be diverse,

including "my kids grew up here," "I built this home," or "I don't want to leave the school district or neighborhood." The strength of the Friendly's desire and commitment to keep the house will be critical to the potential Investor. Why? The desire to keep the home gives the Friendly a strong incentive to purchase the home from the Investor as soon as possible after the auction. That desire will motivate the Friendly to repair and maintain the property in the meantime.

3. ***Financially Qualified.*** It's essential that the financial problems which put the Friendlies in foreclosure be behind them, and they can afford to make new house payments. That doesn't necessarily mean their financial situation has recovered 100%—for many it won't. The financially recovered Friendly who experienced divorce or death of a spouse may not be a two-income household again, but they may be employed with a steady job with the ability to afford a reduced mortgage payment. The financially recovered Friendly whose company went under in the aftermath of the real estate crash may not have a booming company again; she may have a full-time job with less income, but enough to make reduced house payments. The financially recovered Friendly whose cancer is now in remission may still not be working but may now be old enough to draw on social security and pension plans to replace much of the loss in income.

As a Friendly, expect that the Investor will request to see your monthly budget, prior year tax returns, bank statements, pay stubs, and other financial information to evaluate your ability to afford to stay in the home. Your hesitation or unwillingness to provide financial information can be a suspicious and unwelcome red flag. Keep in mind the Investor knows you had financial problems but needs to know you are now sufficiently recovered and capable of affording to stay in the home. The Investor appreciates any financial or other information you can provide to support your claim to be able to afford the home. Seek to provide more than requested, not to hide or refuse to provide financial information. Consider any other information that would be helpful to the Investors, such as contributions from family members who may be willing to continue with their financial assistance.

4. **Decent Condition of the Home.** Experienced foreclosure Investors know that people in foreclosure are unaware if they'll be able to keep their home, and therefore don't maintain the house as they otherwise would. If a Friendly in foreclosure gets a leak in the roof, it would be financially foolish to put a new roof on the home. More likely, the owner will put a bucket under the leak. However, the Investor needs to evaluate the house and may use a home inspector before agreeing to bid on it. The Investor may also bring an appraiser or local real estate broker. After the auction, we recommend any costs to repair or maintain the home be added to the Purchase Option price unless the Friendly is doing the work. A house in decent condition with few necessary repairs will be highly attractive to the Investor, not just on the surface but because the level of care for the property typically corresponds to the Friendly's level of attachment to the home and the likelihood that they will exercise the purchase option in the lease.

Before meeting with an Investor, prepare your home as best you can. Be honest and forthright with the Investor about any problems with the home. Expressing desire and presenting a plan to repair and maintain problem areas in the future can go a long way.

5. ***Friendly!*** Potential Investors especially want to help nice families. That's human nature and is one of the two main reasons Investors invest in Foreclosure Friendlies. Many conventional landlords wouldn't even consider renting to someone after foreclosure, much less buying a foreclosed home, because of a Friendly's recent financial history. Investors are taking a significant risk in buying and leasing the property to someone who was just in foreclosure. Investors want to know what kind of relationship they will have with a future tenant before committing to a lease. Being nice isn't insignificant. A Friendly who is pleasant, open and honest, forthright, and cooperative is very appealing to an Investor. An adversarial or begrudging start will quickly lead to the end of an otherwise potentially successful Friendly Foreclosure.

Please treat Friendlies with respect and kindness, as the world has been kicking them around a lot lately. You're their knight in shining armor, and they'll undoubtedly treat you well. Reciprocity can also have a great ROI! Arrogance and rudeness only breed hostility, and that is not the kind of relationship you want to foster with a new tenant. If successful with this strategy, your relationship with the Friendly won't just be as landlord and tenant or seller and buyer. You saved their home and maybe even their marriage and family! You gave their kids a chance to stay in their home in the neighborhood in which they grew up. They'll be able to finish school where they started. The family will be incredibly thankful for what you've done, and rightfully so. They'll likely be grateful and cooperative during the entire length of your business relationship and beyond.

Chapter 8: Finding Foreclosure Friendlies

6. *Mortgage Pre-qualified.* A mortgage pre-qualification letter is strong support for the Friendly's ability to repurchase the home after the auction. This is very attractive to an Investor. Flippers would love to hear that a Friendly can get a new mortgage in a year or less. Holders are happy enough if it takes you three years after the foreclosure to get a mortgage, and sometimes it does.

Friendlies will have to consult with good mortgage brokers to determine their ability and timing to secure a new mortgage. Make sure you consult with a few brokers to get a good consensus. Mortgage brokers want to say "yes" and tend to do so, sometimes to find out later the real answer is "no" or "not yet".

7. *Mortgage Pre-qualification of an After-Auction Buyer!* Most lenders won't approve foreclosed homeowners for a mortgage to buy their former home back for at least a year after the court concludes the foreclosure case. However, one terrific scenario, which you saw in the earlier Flip examples, is when an Investor will purchase the home for cash at the auction, rent it to the Friendly for a few months while a friend or relative, the "After-Auction Buyer," is getting a conventional mortgage to buy the house back. A Friendly who has a willing After-Auction Buyer will be simply irresistible to Investors. That After-Auction Buyer gives the Investor confidence to bid higher at the auction for a smaller but quicker profit. That gives the Friendlies a better chance of keeping their home.

8. *Low-Bid Mortgage Lender.* If the mortgage being foreclosed is a VA or FHA mortgage, the likelihood of the Friendly's mortgage servicer/bank bidding low at the auction is good. That's true today also if Fannie Mae or Freddie Mac owns the mortgage. It may appear, for

example, that Bank of America owns the mortgage because that's where the Friendly got it or sends her mortgage payments. However, most large banks, like Bank of America, sell approximately 100% of their mortgages on the secondary mortgage market, and Fannie and Freddie buy a large share of the mortgages on the secondary mortgage market. The actual ownership of the mortgage loan is vital information for the Investor because it provides significant insight that is usually not published elsewhere. More than half the mortgages in this country are VA, FHA, Fannie Mae, or Freddie Mac. Friendlies should find out if their mortgage is part of this critical majority! If it is, they should inform their Investor. That will make their day because now they'll have a good chance of winning at the auction with a relatively low bid.

You can find out if Fannie Mae or Freddie Mac own your mortgage by going to www.knowyouroptions.com/loanlookup or ww3.freddiemac.com/loanlookup and completing the brief security questions. If the websites say the loan is not Fannie Mae or Freddie Mac, call the mortgage servicer and ask. The sites sometimes say "No" when the correct answer is "Yes" because the answers you provided weren't identical to the information in the database. If you have a low foreclosing first mortgage and underwater second mortgage, as described in paragraph four above, the result should also be a low initial bid.

9. ***Low Foreclosing First Mortgage, Underwater Second Mortgage.*** As noted above, the home must be underwater. However, a homeowner with a small first mortgage and a second mortgage, which together add

Chapter 8: Finding Foreclosure Friendlies

up to more than the market value of the home, can create an attractive situation for an Investor. For example:

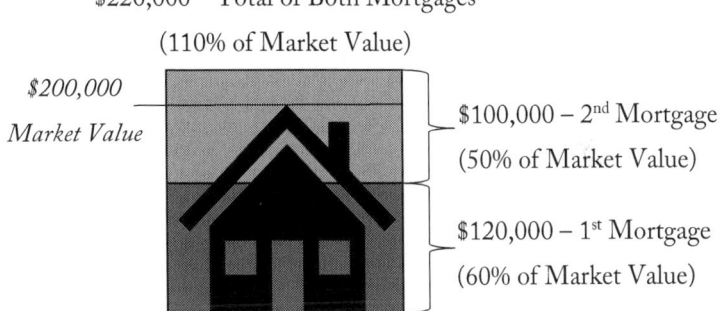

$220,000 – Total of Both Mortgages
(110% of Market Value)

$200,000 Market Value

$100,000 – 2nd Mortgage
(50% of Market Value)

$120,000 – 1st Mortgage
(60% of Market Value)

Generally, a foreclosing lender at an auction cannot make an opening bid more than the amount due to it. Therefore, the first mortgage lender in the above example could open the auction with a maximum bid of $120,000, or 60% of the market value. For various reasons, including the subsequent requirement of paying off the first mortgage, second mortgage lenders usually don't bid at first mortgage auctions. So, there is a good chance a Friendly Investor can win a property in this situation for only $1 over the opening bid, or $120,001. Most often, but not always, the second mortgage does not remain a lien against the home after the first mortgage foreclosure auction. Check with your attorney to be sure.

10. ***The B Word... Bankruptcy.*** In some states, lenders don't hold homeowners personally liable for the mortgage debt on a primary residence, so if you live in one of those states, much of this may not apply to you. However, even if you live in one of those states, a second mortgage on your home, large credit card bills, or other debt may make this section important to you, too.

A Friendly who is not liable for the mortgage debt will therefore not be liable for any deficiency (or difference) between the balance owed on the mortgage and winning auction bid. In such a case, an Investor can rest assured that the Friendly will not be saddled with a substantial financial obligation after the auction, which would render them unable to exercise their Purchase Option.

 All right, don't get upset. Read and understand this essential segment. The Premier Friendly has already filed bankruptcy, or soon will. Yes, I can feel you cringing! "I don't want to do bankruptcy. The thought of it is grotesque to me. I would be mortified if anyone ever knew I declared bankruptcy. What about my credit? Will I ever be able to buy another house? Get another mortgage?" Yes, I've heard all those reactions and more, but this is far too important a topic to dismiss just because it doesn't initially set well with you.

To start with, yes, your credit will recover faster than you would imagine. You'll probably get new credit card offers before you've finished your bankruptcy. You should be able to get a reasonable mortgage in about one to three years, or maybe sooner, depending on your circumstances, such as income, credit history after the bankruptcy, monthly expenses, and debt ratios.

You're not the only one. Bankruptcy is a useful financial tool utilized by some of the most sophisticated investors in the world! It's nothing for which you should be ashamed. It's a practical solution to a sometimes extremely complex set of problems. By declaring bankruptcy, you'll be joining a large, often sophisticated and elite club, which includes wildly successful people from Walt Disney to President Donald Trump!

Chapter 8: Finding Foreclosure Friendlies

Bankruptcy is a right for which you bought and paid. *Every time you make a mortgage payment or a credit card payment or a payment of any type that includes interest, you are paying for the right to declare bankruptcy. Lenders factor in the cost of bankruptcy when determining their interest rates. You've been paying for this right your entire adult life. Don't lose any sleep over any money your bank or credit card companies might lose. They'll be OK, and you will, too.*

Bankruptcy may buy you several additional free months in your home. *In Illinois, filing bankruptcy at the right time can delay your foreclosure auction by 2–4 months or more. That timeframe may be similar in your state. The rent you save by not moving or completing the Foreclosure Friendly sooner should more than cover the cost of bankruptcy by giving you an extra few months to reside free in your home.*

However, if you wait until after the foreclosure auction, the bankruptcy will buy you little, if any, additional time in your home. It will become a cost, probably a significant cost, that you may be forced to pay while you're also paying rent every month for your tiny new apartment on the poor side of town.

Bankruptcy may be forced upon you by the foreclosure. *In Illinois, after the auction, courts routinely assess personal deficiency judgments to foreclosure property homeowners. These deficiency judgments are often tens of thousands or even hundreds of thousands of dollars, and occasionally even more substantial. That substantial deficiency judgment can follow you around for a lifetime. Can you imagine? After the bank repossesses your home and evicts you and your family, it sends you a massive bill, followed by collection agencies chasing you. What a* nightmare! This probable outcome may force bankruptcy upon you after a foreclosure is over.

If that is the case, and if you qualify, you may want to file bankruptcy before the foreclosure auction. That will eliminate the risk of a personal deficiency judgment while allowing you to stay in your home at no additional cost for additional months. Note that in some states, your mortgage servicer may not be permitted to obtain a personal deficiency judgment against you. In those states, bankruptcy may not be necessary but would likely buy you additional time in the home if it is desirable and if you file for bankruptcy before the auction.

Bankruptcy impact on credit. You're already in foreclosure. You could add Bankruptcy to it, put more or all your money problems behind you at the same time, and start building your financial future, starting with a few more free months in your home. In some respects, bankruptcy will improve your credit, as it eliminates debt and improves credit ratios.

Follow that bankruptcy and foreclosure auction with a Foreclosure Friendly lease and subsequent re-purchase of your home, and your life may look diametrically different in just a year or two!

The Premier Foreclosure Friendly

The Premier Friendly will draw more Investors and inspire them to work harder and bid higher to partner with them to save their home.

If you can characterize your property as a Premier Foreclosure Friendly, you should be able to significantly increase your odds of keeping your home under favorable terms.

Chapter 8: Finding Foreclosure Friendlies

The Premier Foreclosure Friendly is a little different for a flipper than for a holder.

For a flipper, the Premier Foreclosure Friendly Homeowner:

- Had a financial hardship but can now demonstrate the hardship has passed and he or she can afford to keep the home.
- Has a home worth less than the balance due on the mortgages attached to the property.
- Is likely to have a low opening bid at the auction either due to a 1) low foreclosing first mortgage with an underwater second mortgage; 2) a Fannie Mae or Freddie Mac or FHA or VA mortgage, or 3) a published bid less than the maximum bid determined by the Friendly Investor.
- Has an After-Auction Buyer, typically a spouse (not on the deed or mortgage) or relative or close friend who has been pre-approved for a mortgage to purchase the property in foreclosure from the Investor at the fair market value after the Investor wins the Auction.
- Is friendly!

For a holder, the Premier Foreclosure Friendly Homeowner:

- Had a financial hardship but who can now demonstrate the hardship has passed.
- Can afford rent that provides a 10% or greater return on the Investor winning bid, net of the Investor's real estate tax, insurance, and homeowner assessment costs.
- Has a valid and reasonable opinion of the current fair market value of the home in good condition.

- Is likely to have a low opening bid at the auction either due to a 1) low foreclosing first mortgage with an underwater second mortgage; 2) a Fannie Mae or Freddie Mac or FHA or VA mortgage, or 3) a published bid less than the maximum bid determined by the Friendly Investor.
- Is committed to keeping the home and has medium or long-term ties to the house and the community, such as a desire to see the children finish high school in a few years in that district.
- Has previously filed bankruptcy and has little or no debt.
- Has been pre-approved, from an income perspective, for a mortgage to eventually re-purchase the home, but must wait a year or longer after the foreclosure or bankruptcy to get that mortgage.
- Has a home in relatively good condition, with plans to repair or decorate, when the Friendly knows he or she will be able to keep the home.
- Is friendly!

The flipper Investor will be less picky about the rent, the condition of the home, or the current owner's ability to get a mortgage in the future. Those are of little consequence if the flippers know they'll be able to sell the home to a relative or friend of the Friendly right after the auction. Alternatively, the holder will be pickier about rent and the condition of the home. Holders may also provide less pressure to exercise the Purchase Option.

The two Friendly Foreclosure Flips described in Chapter Four both provided spectacular profits quickly to the Investors. Note that the second example was a Premier Foreclosure Friendly. The other was not because it didn't have an FHA, VA, Fannie Mae, or Freddie Mac mortgage. The

Chapter 8: Finding Foreclosure Friendlies

lesson to be learned is that the Friendly does not have to be a Premier Foreclosure Friendly before the auction to result in spectacular profits after the auction.

Chapter 6: Determining and Negotiating Terms

The Lease with Rider

When debating or negotiating terms between Investor and Friendly, this chapter offers guidance for fair and equitable terms for both parties.

Investors, consider your potential attractive returns when the Friendly needs more affordable terms. Friendlies, appreciate the value the Investor brings to the table and the possibility of keeping your home. Then do your level best to provide reasonable terms to that Investor.

Friendlies and Investors, try to think of yourselves as teammates. You're working together to win the game. **Competing too ambitiously with each other could result in both of you losing unnecessarily.**

The primary document for the Friendly Foreclosure transaction will be a Lease with a Rider. The Investor will generally provide a standard form of Lease, consistent with any local regulations. The Investor may want to contact a local attorney about preparing the Lease with Rider. The Rider will include the Purchase Option terms, the maximum price to which the Investor agrees to bid at the auction, a provision about repairs and maintenance, and any other non-standard Lease provisions.

Terms of the Friendly Foreclosure Transaction

Market Value. The first step is to determine the "finished fair market value" of the home, which we use as the market value. Determining this value is an important step. We look at Zillow, Eppraisal, the local MLS, the Tax Assessor's value, and any other available sources. Zillow is usually the first and easiest value to find, and it is the value everyone else sees, so we pay much attention to it. Other potential auction bidders may use Zillow as their basis for estimating market value. If it is a reasonable approximation, we'll use the Zillow value as the market value. If the Investors like, they may pay for a formal appraisal on the home. Please don't worry too much about drilling down the fair market value to the nearest penny. The nature of the transaction doesn't require that. At best, even when done by "experts," appraising is an inexact process: part science and part art. Investors and Friendlies will both derive exceptional financial benefits by just being reasonable with each other on all terms. It should not be an adversarial process.

Purchase Option Price. The initial market value determined above will also be the Purchase Option price. We put this provision in a Rider to the Lease. The Friendly may exercise this Option at any time during the term of the lease or any extensions. We increase our Purchase Option price by 3% per year to keep pace with inflation and to provide the Friendly with additional incentive to buy sooner rather than later.

Friendlies, understand that the market value/Purchase Option price will have a significant effect on the maximum amount the Investor will bid at the auction. The higher the Option price (and therefore rent), the higher the Investor will be agreeable to bid, and thus the higher the probability for success at the auction. Many Friendlies feel compelled to negotiate the Purchase Option down but may be losing their home in the process by unnecessarily reducing the Investor's max bid at the auction.

Maximum Bid Price. For our clients, we're able to research the bidding history of foreclosure plaintiffs/banks, thereby determining the likelihood of success of auction bids at various levels. Investors or Friendlies may not

Chapter 8: Finding Foreclosure Friendlies

be able to do that. Bidding practices also vary significantly from county to county in the Chicago area, and we can research those statistics, too.

To give you a general idea of the likelihood of success of a bid, we looked at a random sample of 501 Auctions in the Chicago and suburban counties in 2018. We found:

- Bids up to 70% of the Zillow estimated market value had a 44% chance of winning, almost even odds.
- Bids up to 75% of the Zillow estimated market value had a 57% chance of winning, better than even odds.
- Bids up to 80% of the Zillow estimated market value had a 68% chance of winning, or better than two out of three odds of success. Those are pretty good odds of keeping a home, and that's the bid to which Friendlies want Investors to commit.

We request all our Investors to commit to bidding a minimum of 70%, and we prefer they commit to 75% or above to give our clients better than a 50% chance of keeping their home. The Investors' bidding decision will depend on their impressions of the Friendly and the property, as well as the monthly rent and Purchase Option. Investors should disclose to Friendlies the maximum amount of their bid and state it in the Lease with Rider.

Consider the two Flips discussed in Chapter 4. Both were high bids:

- Example #1 – the Investor bid 77% of the estimated market value.
- Example #2 - the Investor bid 74% of the estimated market value.

The magnitude of these foreclosure flip bids, at 77% and 74%, demonstrates how much higher an Investor can go with a Friendly Foreclosure flip than with a conventional foreclosure auction purchase. An investor bidding 74% or 77% at a conventional foreclosure auction would be lucky to break even after 6–12 months of work and waiting after the auctions. In the examples in this book, the Friendly Investors made stellar profits in less than three months, not withstanding their relatively high auction bids.

As discussed in Chapter 2, the estimated breakeven point for investors buying conventional foreclosure auction properties is 75% of estimated market value. To make a reasonable profit, most experienced foreclosure auction bidders won't bid more than 65% of market value.

However, Friendly Investors have much lower costs. They typically don't pay real estate brokerage commissions, thereby saving closing costs of about 5%. They also don't have repairs and renovation or holding expenses, saving 10–20%; let's call it 15%. Total costs for a Foreclosure Friendly Investor might only amount to 5–10% of the market value, making the breakeven auction price 90 – 95% of the market value. **Let's say the Foreclosure Friendly breakeven auction price is 90% of the fair market value of the property,** compared to the conventional investor breakeven auction price of 75%.

Consider the charts in Table 5. After winning with a bid of 75% of the estimated market value at an auction, a conventional foreclosure investor wouldn't make a profit, but a Friendly Investor would make a 15% profit. That's a significant difference.

Differences in breakeven point is a critical matter, so please understand and remember it. This difference gives a Friendly Investor a considerable advantage over a conventional investor when bidding at the auction. A Friendly Investor can bid up to 90% of the market value of the home and still break-even. Of course, the Investor doesn't usually buy Friendly

Chapter 8: Finding Foreclosure Friendlies

Conventional Foreclosure Auction

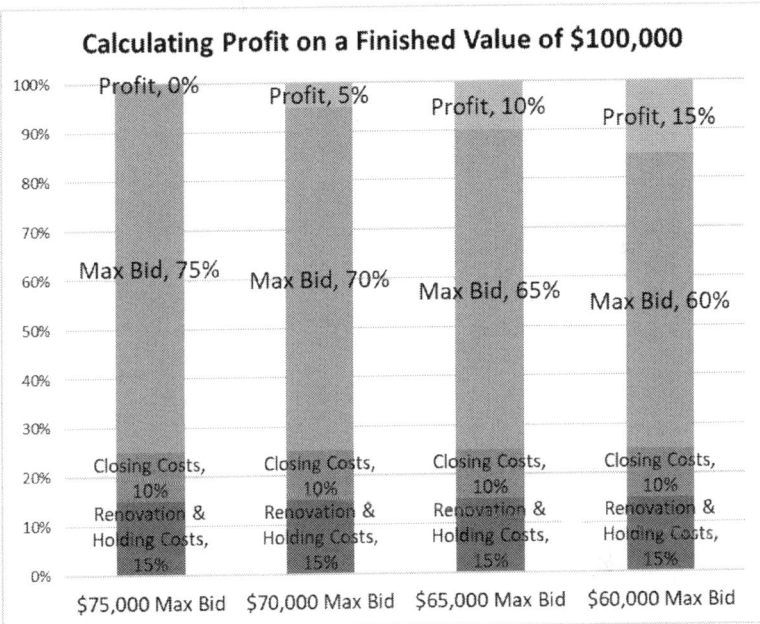

Friendly Foreclosure Auction

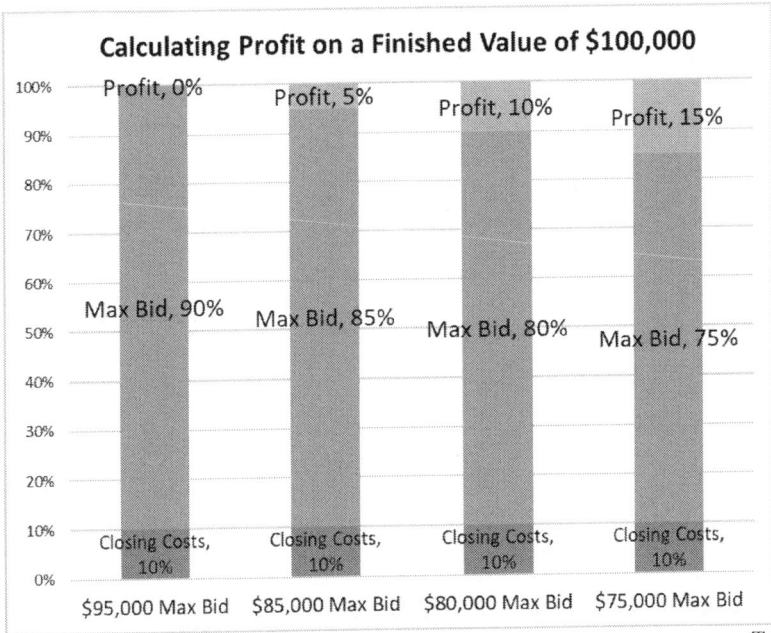

Table 5

Foreclosures to break-even, unless the Investor is Mom or Dad, doing it for the benefit of the kids, without an eye toward profit.

 The other vitally important point to remember from this analysis is that you can make terrific profits when paying upwards of 80% of the market value of a home at a Foreclosure Friendly flip auction. So, Investors, don't be too conservative when determining your bid. Remember, worst case, you'll still own the bricks and mortar if you win the bid. And if buying a home for 80% of market value or less is the worst investment you ever make, you're going to be a very successful investor.

 If your mortgage is FHA, VA, Fannie Mae, or Freddie Mac, the opening bid will likely be relatively low. That's an essential piece of information for you to share with your potential Investor. Find out! Few auction bidders, other than your Investor, will bid 70% of market value or higher. If your Investor has agreed to bid 70% or higher, the biggest threat of losing the auction comes from the initial bid by the foreclosure plaintiff, the bank. As the bank gets a "credit bid" and doesn't have to put any money on the table at the auction; the foreclosure plaintiff may bid up to the full amount due on the mortgage. If the mortgage is FHA, VA, Fannie Mae, or Freddie Mac, there is a good chance the opening bid by the plaintiff will be less than 70% of market value.

Published Bids. Some sheriffs and auctioneers and law firms representing foreclosure plaintiffs publish the opening bid before the auction. Some bids are published just hours or minutes before the auction. Some are published days or weeks before the auction. Be sure to check with your sheriff, auctioneer, or plaintiff law firm, usually through their website, to find out if you can get the opening bid before the auction. That will help everyone be better prepared, and it may allow for some last minute negotiated changes between Friendly and Investor to enable the Friendly Foreclosure strategy to work.

For example, the opening bid might be $301,000 on a property for which the Investor had only intended to bid up to $300,000. In that case, the Investor and Friendly might well decide to bid up to $301,001 with just a slight adjustment to rent and possibly to the Purchase Option price.

Rent. We use the maximum bid price to determine the rent while looking at the previous mortgage payment for guidance. We don't like to be higher than the prior mortgage payment if that wasn't affordable. In addition, we also consider local rents, but mostly to be sure our rent isn't too high.

We try to get the Investor a rent return on investment between 6% and 10%. So, if the maximum Investor bid at an auction will be $100,000, we want the rent to include $6,000-$10,000 per year in return, which equates to $500-$833 per month. We add an estimated amount to reimburse the Investor for Real Estate Taxes, Homeowners Insurance, and Assessments if any.

So, if those all add up to $2,400 per year, then we add $200 per month to the rent. That would suggest a rent of $700- 1,033, ($500 + $200 to $833 + $200), per month. That's a broad range.

Investors, please don't be too tough on your rent negotiations. You want to get a good return, but you should strive for affordability for the Friendly, as your big payoff will come on the resale of the home.

Friendlies, be reasonable. Of course, you want a low rent, but you want the Investor to bid as high as possible at the auction so you have the best chance of keeping your home. Friendlies, don't lose your home at the auction because you got your Investor to agree to a low monthly rent when you could have and would have paid more to stay there.

Friendlies should pay all utilities, maintenance, and any other fees or expenses associated with the home. Any amounts the Investor pays will increase the Purchase Option price accordingly.

We recommend rent increases of 5% per year to keep pace with local rental rates and to provide the Friendly with additional incentive to buy sooner rather than later.

Finally, we establish the rent, in writing, before the auction. If the Investor is successful in buying for a lower price at the auction, we do not reduce the rent accordingly. That is a higher profit opportunity for Investors if they are lucky at the auction. We want to give this opportunity and encouragement to bring in the Investors. If the Investor makes a last-minute decision to bid higher at the auction, rent doesn't go up because of that decision.

Lease Term. Normally, we ask our Investors to agree to a three-year lease. It may take that long for a Friendly to get a new mortgage after a foreclosure. Also, because the foreclosure sometimes doesn't officially end until months after the auction, the Investor should add that period to the lease term. So, when I refer to a three-year lease, if it takes three months to dismiss the foreclosure, the lease term should be for three years and three months. Investors should be flexible to make sure the Friendly will later be able to obtain a mortgage, which should be the goal of both parties.

Note also that many mortgage brokers like to say "YES" when reality says otherwise. I can't tell you how many times a mortgage broker has told a client that he could get a mortgage for her within a short time after the

Chapter 8: Finding Foreclosure Friendlies

auction, only to find out later he couldn't. So, you Investors and Friendlies, be careful when mortgage brokers tell you they can get a mortgage the day after the auction, or even a year after the auction. I'm not disparaging mortgage brokers, as they're usually just overanxious to help, but there are many mortgage rules which may apply to those fresh out of foreclosure or bankruptcy. Friendlies must make sure their broker knows their foreclosure and bankruptcy situation and that they're asking about a mortgage to buy the house lost in foreclosure.

 Friendlies should note that many Investors will prefer a quicker payoff. So, if you or a friend or family member can get a mortgage and repurchase the home after just a few months, then that will make the transaction MUCH more desirable to many Investors. A 6 or 12-month Lease would be very attractive to an Investor, who could then bid higher at the auction to buy that Friendly Foreclosure. So, if you can do shorter, say so and do it! If not, go long. Many holder Investors will be happy enough doing a three-year deal, and maybe even longer if you ask.

Repairs and Maintenance. A Friendly Foreclosure transaction is a strategy for the Friendly to keep the home. We want the Friendly to care for and maintain the house as their own, and that's usually what the Friendly wants. In our Lease with Riders, we add a provision stating any expenditures for repairs or maintenance made by the Investor will be added to the Purchase Option price. If in the middle of the winter the furnace goes out, and a new one will cost $3,000, Friendlies have two choices. They can replace it and pay for it themselves, or they can call the Investor to replace it. That cost of replacement will then be added to the Purchase Option price. A Friendly can't ask the Investor to spend $3,000 on a new furnace right before exercising the Purchase Option price and expect no adjustment in purchase price.

Payment of Rent and Security Deposit. Although both parties should sign a Lease before the auction, no money should change hands until after the auction. The Friendly should be prepared to pay the rent, perhaps the prorated first month and the entire last months' rent, or a security deposit, the day after the auction. The Investors may not be the legal title owner of the property the day after the auction, but they will be the equitable owners, and therefore it is appropriate for the Investors to begin receiving rent on the day after the auction. We put that provision in all our Lease Riders.

Although we recommend no money change hands before the auction, an Investor may ask for the initial rent payment and security deposit, if any, to be paid and held in escrow by an attorney before the auction. The attorney would distribute the funds to the Investor or Friendly right after the auction, depending on the outcome. We don't recommend this, but it's not an unreasonable compromise by the Investor.

We ask our Friendlies to pay a prorated rent for the month of the auction, along with the last month of rent for the lease on the day after the auction. We don't like security deposits for various technical legal reasons. After the initial rent payment, rent is due on the first of every month, and there is a 5% penalty if paid after the fifth day of the month.

Documents and Pre-Auction Work to be Done by Investors

Following are several items that Investors need to take care of before the Foreclosure Auction:

Chapter 8: Finding Foreclosure Friendlies

Lease with a Rider. The primary documentation for a Foreclosure Friendly transaction is a Lease with a Rider. Local residential lease regulations vary considerably, so a sample is not included in this book. However, finding and completing a local residential lease form is not a difficult task. For our Foreclosure Friendly Leases in Illinois, we add a Rider with certain provisions unique to the transaction. Following are provisions normally included in our Riders:

1. This lease is contingent upon Lessor's successful bid at the applicable foreclosure auction on _____ 20___.

2. Lessor agrees to bid up to $_____ at the applicable foreclosure auction, if necessary.

3. Upon Lessor's success at the foreclosure auction, Lessee shall promptly pay, in advance, prorated rent for _(month of auction)_, 20___ in the amount of $_____, plus $_____ for _(last month of lease)_, 20___ for a total of $_____.

4. Both parties understand that Lessor hereunder may not be the legal, technical owner of the subject property, as of the auction date. However, in consideration of the mutual promises and benefits herein, Lessor hereunder shall be recognized and treated by Lessee hereunder as the equitable owner of the subject property and Lessee shall abide by all terms hereunder beginning _(date of auction)_, 20___.

5. Rent shall increase by 5% on each first day of the month following the anniversary of this lease.

6. Lessee is hereby granted an option to purchase the subject premises at any time, up to and including __(last day of lease and all extensions)__ , so long as Lessee is not in default and remains an occupant of the property under this Lease with Lessor, under the following terms:

    A. Option Purchase Price shall be __(market value of property on date of auction)__ ,

    B. Option Purchase Price shall increase by _3%_ on each anniversary of this Lease;

    C. Terms of the purchase by Lessee shall be consistent with the then current local Multi-Board Residential Real Estate Contract except there shall be no prorations for real estate taxes not yet due. This is in recognition of prior year's real estate taxes incurred by Buyer hereunder but paid by Seller hereunder after Seller's initial property acquisition. There shall be no homeowner's association or other prorations for periods in which the Seller/Lessor hereunder did not own the property.

7. Lessee hereby affirmatively states the Premises and contents will be well maintained during the term of this lease and any extension, and no improvements on or about the Premises shall be intentionally removed or

damaged, regardless of who originally provided the items or work to improve them.

8. If Lessee elects not to purchase the Premises, Lessee shall vacate the Premises at the expiration of this Lease, leaving it in good, broom-clean condition, with all fixtures, appliances and window treatments remaining in the premises, also in good condition, normal wear and tear excepted.

9. The cost of all maintenance and repairs requested by Lessee and paid by Lessor shall be added to the Option Purchase Price.

10. After exercising the option to purchase, the Buyer will cooperate and sign necessary documents to allow the Seller to accomplish a tax-free exchange, if requested. The Seller shall bear all associated costs, if any, to accomplish the exchange.

11. In the event the Lessor wins the applicable auction, but for whatever reason does not subsequently obtain title to the property, and can therefore not honor this lease, the Lease shall be null and void, and all rent received by Lessor in excess of $500.00 shall be returned to the Lessee.

In the event the Lessee runs a business out of the home, such as a child care center, we add the following provision:

12. Lessee shall maintain insurance in type and sufficient amount, in the Lessor's sole and reasonable discretion,

at Lessee's cost, on all business operations in the home. Lessee must name Lessor as an additional insured in all policies.

Assess the Title. A clear understanding of the condition of the title is essential. I repeat this from a prior chapter because it is so important you understand and heed this caution. The condition of the title will be influenced by the state in which the property is located. Investors can't assume all liens, other mortgages, homeowner association liens, mechanics liens, delinquent taxes, and judgments will be removed when they receive the sheriff's deed after the auction.

We have seen it time and again where a conventional investor buys a property at auction only to find out afterwards that there is a priority lienholder who must be paid off or the new investor will risk losing the property in a 2nd foreclosure by the 1st lienholder!

Mistakes in this area could easily cost you tens, or even hundreds, of thousands of dollars. An experienced real estate attorney should be able to assist you with this assessment. I recommend getting a formal title commitment before buying at the auction. If successful at the auction, you should buy the title insurance policy. Check real estate taxes, homeowner association fees, other mortgages, and all title matters.

Don't forget homeowners insurance! Arrange for a homeowners insurance "binder" before the auction. Investors should start the policy on the day they win the auction. From that point on, they have an insurable interest, notwithstanding the fact they may not have legal title to the property. Investors will have equitable title. If the Investor doesn't insure the property from the day of the auction, probably nobody will. **If the auctioned home is destroyed after the Investor paid for it at the auction,**

the auction price will not be refunded! I've seen a home completely destroyed after the Investor won the auction but failed to insure the property. It happens.

If the Friendly owner is currently maintaining a homeowners insurance policy, the Investor might be added to that policy as an additional insured. Check with the insurance agent before the auction.

Evaluate the Property. Investors probably wouldn't consider buying real estate without first inspecting it. With conventional foreclosure auction properties, prior auctions usually aren't an option. With Friendly Foreclosure auctions, they are! So Investors, take advantage.

> *Have a good look at the property. If necessary, bring an inspector or someone who has a good understanding of home construction and values. If the home needs a new roof, be sure to discuss that with the homeowner. Let the homeowners know that you could pay for a new roof and add it on to their Purchase Option price, or they could pay for it with no addition to the Purchase Option price. Have those discussions before the auction, if possible.*

Summary

Negotiations should be a joint effort to come to affordable resolutions for the Friendlies and profitable resolutions for the Investors. Remember, you are on the same team – so work to keep negotiations positive, reasonable, and friendly. Being thoroughly prepared before the auction is the key which sets a Friendly Foreclosure transaction apart from a conventional foreclosure investment. This isn't the type of deal to do on a handshake basis or to negotiate after the fact. Everything should be in writing and signed before the Auction.

Chapter 7: Finding a Friendly Investor

I must start by complimenting you Friendlies. You're not laying down and letting the world walk all over you. You're fighting back for yourselves and probably your family. You're not giving up during this difficult time. You're searching for a solution and you're willing to put in the work necessary to find one. I tip my hat to you!

The Premier Investor

When considering an Investor, homeowners must be cautious. Some might try to take advantage of distressed homeowners. Be on guard, go slow (OK, not too slow as auctions are not slowing down), and be cautious.[7]

Following are qualities I would recommend and questions to ask when considering a potential Investor:

The Premier Investor:

- Will have read the ForeclosureFriendlies.com book and will understand and agree to the concept and goals of the program.
- May have experience with real estate investment or Foreclosure Friendlies, but that is not mandatory.
- Will have a valid and reasonable opinion of market value of the home in good condition.

---

[7] If you move forward with any of these strategies, as always, consult with a local attorney or tax advisor – this book is not meant to be legal or tax advice. And yes, if your home is in the Chicago area, you are welcome to call me, and I may be able to help you find a Premier Investor.

- Will agree to bid up to 80% of the estimated market value at the auction – 75% is good but doesn't qualify for the "Premier" category. (See Chapter Four examples of bids at 77% and 74% of market value.)
- Will have the financial wherewithal combined with the experience or ability to complete a Foreclosure Friendly transaction. In Illinois, that means the Investor must be able to come up with the entire bid price within 24-48 hours of the auction, depending on the auctioneer. A few auctions require 100% of the bid at the auction.
- Will provide a Lease and Rider, with a fair, affordable rent and Purchase Price Option along with even-handed terms consistent with the recommendations in this book.
- Will be respectful, flexible, and reasonable with the Friendlies and their family.

Important Questions to Ask an Investor

As the Investor will want to see your home and learn about you, you'll want to also learn about the Investor. Be sure you get clear answers to these questions before the auction. After the auction, your leverage and negotiating power will be diminished. It won't be eliminated, but it will be significantly reduced. Your Investor will make a far higher return if you stay in the home and do your part, rather than leave. Still, your leverage is strongest before the auction.

Have you ever bought a Friendly Foreclosure property? It would be great if the Investors already own Foreclosure Friendly properties, or if they currently own other rental properties, but Friendlies shouldn't disqualify them if they don't. This auction purchase might be the Investor's first real estate investment. That's OK. Working together, you'll both make it a great one!

Have you read the ForeclosureFriendlies.com book? An Investor who read the book and understands and agrees with the program is your best option. Just because you found the Investor on the ForeclosureFriendlies.com website doesn't mean that Investor read the book or understands the program. Make sure he or she does!

Are you a flipper or a holder? Knowing this answer will give the Friendly a better sense of the goals of the Investor. If they are flippers, the Investors will want someone to repurchase the home as soon as possible. A holder will be far less concerned with the buyback date, as long as the Friendly is paying rent on a timely basis.

What will be my Purchase Option price? Friendlies and their Investors will determine the Purchase Option price before the auction. We look at Zillow, the Tax Assessor's estimated market value, and broker opinions of value/comparative market analyses. Occasionally, the Investors will want to do a formal appraisal at their own cost. Market value may be somewhat negotiable between the Friendly and the Investors. Please keep in mind, the lower the agreed market value, the lower the Purchase Option price. That sounds good to the Friendly, but the lower the Purchase Option price, the lower the Investor will bid at the auction, and the smaller the chance for success of this strategy. If a Friendly convinces the Investor that their home is only worth $90,000, rather than $100,000, the Investor's maximum bid at the auction (which assumes 75% of estimated market value), will drop from $75,000 to $67,500. That's a significant drop which could result in the Friendly losing the home for which she would happily have paid $100,000 rather than losing it and being forced to move out quickly. Friendlies, please be careful not to be too tight in your negotiations with the Investor, who is trying to help you. Be reasonable with rent and purchase option negotiations.

Will my Purchase Option price increase? We recommend our Investors increase the Purchase Option Price by 3% per year. Keep in mind, this is an option and not a requirement, so it can only run in favor of the Friendly. If the price is too high, the Friendly doesn't have to use the Option. If home prices are quickly escalating in the area, and the Option Price is lower than the home value, the Investor will not be permitted to cancel the Option or increase the price. That means the Friendly might be able to repurchase their home in the future at less than the market value at that time.

Up to what percentage of the fair market value/Purchase Option price will you bid? The Investor should go up to a minimum bid of 70% of fair market value of the home in good condition. It's preferable that the Investor go even higher, e.g., 75% or 80%. Note the Investor must be confident the Friendlies will stay in the home and keep up their end of the bargain. The Investors must also believe they purchased the house at a price at which they can sell it and recoup the investment along with some reasonable profit if the Friendlies don't exercise the Purchase Option or continue renting.

What will be my rent? The Foreclosure Friendlies with whom I work often want to pay the lowest possible rent. Who doesn't? Usually, their first reflex is to try to negotiate the lowest possible rent from the Investor. That's usually not a great idea. The lower the rent, the more difficult it will be to find a good Investor, and the lower the Investor will bid at the

Chapter 7: Finding a Friendly Investor

Important Message to Friendlies and Investors

Friendlies, don't let this paragraph scare or deter you. It's just a warning to use reasonable caution. Obviously, an Investor will want to see the home before the auction. That's one of the primary benefits of the Friendly Foreclosure strategy. A danger in this strategy is that a potential Investor may decide he wants that home for himself, and not for the purpose of saving it for the current homeowners. The Friendly Foreclosure strategy minimizes that risk because the financial return is much higher for the Investor. Although the danger is minimized, it is not completely eliminated. There may be some potential Investors without scruples that would use the strategy as a pretense to gain access and inspect the property before the auction for their own selfish purposes. In my opinion, anyone who would deceive and take advantage of distressed homeowners in this manner is despicable. Any potential Investor with any such ideas, I urge you to reconsider, and just don't do it. My philosophy is "We all get paid in the end", and you will, too, but I don't want Friendly Homeowners to lose their homes waiting for nefarious Investors to be punished for their evil life deeds. Investors, please don't even consider this! If you're really not interested in the program or you can't work out a deal with the Friendly Homeowner, just don't bid on that property. There are plenty of other properties out there. I know most investors wouldn't think of doing something like this, and I apologize if I've offended you, but thought it necessary to mention.

Friendly Homeowners, I see the greatest likelihood of the above happening if you're not treating Investors fairly. If you are interviewing dozens of potential Investors and making unreasonable demands, you may be alienating some to the point where they decide they like your home a lot, but they don't like you at all. That could inspire them to bid at the auction for themselves. Remember, be nice and be reasonable. That's the type of family that Friendly Investors will want to help.

auction. For my Foreclosure Friendly clients, I typically suggest the rent amount. Rent must cover real estate taxes, insurance, and association dues, and also provide a return on investment for the Investor. I don't want anyone to get too worried about the math, but let's run through an example for a home valued at $100,000.

1. Real estate taxes, insurance, and homeowner's assessments amount to $2,400 per year or $200 per month for this home.

2. The Investor has agreed to bid a maximum of 75% of the market value of the home, or $75,000, at the foreclosure auction. It's usually that percentage bid or higher to which I ask Investors to commit. It's important the Investor agrees to bid at least 70% of the market value. It's better if he bids up to 80% of market value!

3. To provide a 10% rental return on the investment, 10% of $75,000 is $7,500 per year or $625 per month.

4. Add the $200 in (a) above to the $625 in (c) above for a total monthly rent of $825.

5. For Friendlies who can't afford $825 per month, try reducing the return to the Investor to 9%, then 8%, then 7%, but no lower than 6%. At 8%, rent would be $500 + $200 = $700 per month. At 6%, rent would be $375 + $200 = $575 per month. Yes, those are big differences but remember, it's wise to give the Investor the highest return the Friendly can reasonably afford. Doing so will, hopefully, allow the Friendlies to stay in their home and repurchase it later at a price considerably less than what they now owe on it.

6. The Investor may also want to consider average rents in the area and the current monthly house payment before the foreclosure when

Chapter 7: Finding a Friendly Investor

determining what the new rent should be. The Investor and Friendly should negotiate the lease and Purchase Option before the auction, to confirm that both parties want to proceed under the financial terms.

Will my rent go up? We recommend Investors increase rent by 5% per year. That gives a little more incentive for the Friendly to repurchase their home sooner rather than later, and it makes the home more attractive to an Investor. Real estate investors consist of two main categories: flippers and holders. Holders like to buy real estate, rent it, and hold on to it for the long-term. Holders may be gentler on the annual rent increases because they want Friendlies to stay in the home as renters. Flippers like to buy properties and re-sell them for profit as quickly as possible. They will be more anxious for Friendlies to exercise the Purchase Option, so will try to give them every reason to do so, including higher rent increases.

Who will be responsible for taxes, insurance, repairs, and maintenance? The Investor should pay for taxes, insurance, and any homeowner assessments and will consider those costs when determining rent. Friendlies may want to get renters insurance for their contents. Regarding repairs and maintenance, we advise the Investor to make Friendlies responsible for maintenance and to give them the option to do repairs themselves, with Investor approval, or to request the Investor to do them. Any Investor costs for repairs or maintenance will increase the Purchase Option price accordingly under the recommended Lease terms. Repairs and maintenance done by the Friendly will have no impact on the Purchase Option price.

Will you be preparing the Lease and Purchase Option documents? When will we all sign those? These should be completed, agreed to, and signed before the auction and will only be enforceable if the Investor wins the auction.

When will you make a decision? How much notice of your choice will you give me before the auction? Friendlies need time to identify an alternative Investor if this one decides not to go forward with their home for any reason. Those reasons are diverse and may be utterly unrelated to them or their home. A sudden downturn in the Investor's stock portfolio may make it impossible for them to bid the price initially intended.

How to Find a Friendly Foreclosure Investor

How did you find this book? Was it left on your doorstep with a ribbon around it? Was it mailed to you? If so, contact the person who left it for you. Gifting this book is one of the suggestions I make to Investors regarding how to find you! If an Investor found you, you owe it to the Investor to call him or her first. Hopefully, you'll have to look no further. The Investor should be familiar with the concepts and suggested terms of the Friendly Foreclosure strategy. That's an excellent start for you because my recommendations are intended to be terrific for the Investor and the Friendly!

If you're in the Chicago area, call me! Through the years, my firm has accumulated a list of great Investors who have purchased or hope to purchase a Friendly Foreclosure. We may be able to help you identify, negotiate, or close the transaction with a good Investor.

Read Chapter Nine and then subscribe and create a profile at our new website – www.ForeclosureFriendlies.com – designed to help Friendlies and Investors find one another.

Chapter 7: Finding a Friendly Investor

Find your own Investor with this book! If you live in an area where the Friendly Foreclosure concept is not well known, using this book is an option. Do you have a friend or relative who you especially like or trust or who is already investing in real estate or other opportunities, or has the interest and ability to invest? What about a group of friends or family members? Would you be far too shy or embarrassed about revealing your situation or asking for help? <u>Please understand the Investors in this program can make good, and sometimes spectacular, profits</u>. If you advise friends or relatives of your Friendly Foreclosure opportunity, you won't just be asking for help. You will be offering them an exciting, profit-making opportunity. If I read this book and learned my good friend or relative was a Friendly and didn't tell me, I would be extremely disappointed. Of course, we would both be sad to learn that person lost her home when I could have helped her save it.

What's the best way to approach someone? It would be challenging to introduce and explain the Friendly Foreclosure Strategy in casual conversation. There are too many factors and innuendos for someone to understand out of the blue! So, get a fresh copy of this book. Write your name, telephone number, and email address on the inside cover. Add a card or note on small stationery to bookmark Chapters Three and Four. Your card should say something like:

> Karen, I read this book and thought of you. I hope you enjoy it. Please have a look at Chapters Three and Four and let me know what you think about the concept.
>
> Your Friendly, Steve

Drop it in the mail, or better yet, put a ribbon around it and deliver it personally. That should get the potential Investor's attention. Follow up on the book delivery by calling or texting, asking if she read the book, yet, and what she thought of it. Note that if the person to whom you gave the book is unable to help you, there's a good chance she'll know someone else who could, and she'll undoubtedly want to pass along the idea. Ask them to pass along the book, too. (That's why you didn't write your note on the inside cover.) You'll find after reading about it, potential Investors will be excited about the concept, especially if you're a strong Friendly candidate. If you're a Premier Foreclosure Friendly, any Investor should be thrilled to talk to you. I know I would be! Be sure to determine if you're a Premier Foreclosure Friendly before you start looking for an Investor.

Summary

There are lots of individuals and groups who might make great Investors for you. A good Investor might be a family member or close friend. Often those individuals don't have the necessary cash to act as an Investor but joining together as a group can sometimes make that possible. If that's not a possibility for you, seek other Investors. There are many of them out there. Start by listing your home at ForeclosureFriendlies.com, and then do whatever additional research and work it takes to make your opportunity known to a good Investor. It's worth the effort for you and your family.

Chapter 8: Finding Foreclosure Friendlies

Investors, I must start by thanking you. Since 2008, my crusade has been helping responsible people in foreclosure save their homes. I thank you for your interest in helping, and I welcome your alliance. You'll find it a rewarding endeavor from both a financial and philanthropic perspective.

For Investors who have never met any Friendlies or visited their homes, there are a few things they should know in advance. Typically, Friendlies are not scammers or people "gaming" the system to live in their home for as long as possible at no cost. That's what many believe, but those Friendlies who are trying to save their homes do not fit that description at all.

Most often, Friendlies are normal, above average people who ran into severe financial trouble, often through no fault of their own. Their financial hardship might be due to medical problems, college costs, divorce, retirement, relocation of their company, or just the fact their new boss was a jerk. These things happen all the time, and most can probably relate to some of them. I know I can!

These Friendlies are homeowners just like most Investors! They bought and maintained a home, usually for years, and often for decades before they ran into financial difficulties. Typically, these are responsible individuals who had no choice in the circumstances that forced them into foreclosure. Unfortunately, they've had to go to sleep every night for months, if not years, worrying about the sheriff showing up on their doorstep and throwing them and their family out on the street. Yes, it's free, maybe, but what an ugly way to live! I don't think I've had any clients who haven't had nightmares about the process.

Investors must treat Friendlies with respect and kindness, as the world has been kicking them around a lot, lately. Think about it—an Investor is their knight in shining armor! They'll undoubtedly treat them well. I hope Investors reciprocate. If successful with this strategy, an Investor's relationship with the Friendly won't just be as landlord and tenant or seller and buyer. The Investor saved the Friendly's home and maybe even their marriage and family! The Investor gave the Friendly's kids a chance to stay in their home in the neighborhood in which they grew up. They'll be able to finish high school where they started. The family will be incredibly thankful for what the Investor has done, and rightfully so. They'll likely be grateful and cooperative during the entire length of the business relationship, and well beyond.

When visiting the Friendly's home, Investors may notice is it has not been kept up very well. The carpeting is old and worn, and the place needs minor, and sometimes major, repairs and painting, inside and out. Investors should not let that unfairly impact their opinion of the Friendly family. In Illinois, it can often take a year and a half or longer from the first missed mortgage payment to the foreclosure auction. That's a long time for the Friendlies not to know if they'll be able to keep their home or not.

If there is a leak in the roof, the Friendlies are not going to throw a new roof on the house. That would be financially foolish. They are likely going to put a bucket under it. If a faucet doesn't work, the Friendlies may just use a different faucet. That's not the way they maintained the home in the past, nor will it be how they maintain it in the future if the Friendlies know they have a chance of keeping it. Investors must understand this and lower their expectations of the condition and decorating when first visiting a Friendly home.

Chapter 9: ForeclosureFriendlies.com

If the Friendly Foreclosure strategy works, the Friendlies will be happy, even anxious, to start working on all those repairs and decorating matters they tried to ignore in the past. The Friendlies don't enjoy watching their home deteriorate, but financially it doesn't make sense to do otherwise while in foreclosure.

Please note, also, that people in foreclosure are naturally suspicious of anyone claiming to want to help them. They've heard about some of the scams, and about people who would try to "steal" their home. They know some people will only want to see their home, to see its condition before bidding at the auction and evicting them. Of course, I hope that's not the Investor's plan, and the Friendlies do, too, but they will be suspicious. If you've read the preceding chapters, you know your return will be far greater if you utilize the Friendly Foreclosure strategy and keep the Friendly in their home.

How to Find a Foreclosure Friendly

1. *ForeclosureFriendlies.com*. Read Chapter Nine and then create a profile on the website. Check it regularly. The website is designed with the specific purpose of bringing Investors and Friendlies together. The Friendlies on the website will be your best leads. They should know the process and will be actively looking for a capable Investor. Don't be overly concerned about the distance to the Friendlies' homes, as there should be little or no property management involved if all goes according to plan. Only if you can't find suitable Friendlies on the website, look elsewhere, but keep an eye on the website. That's why it's there!

2. ***Other foreclosure listings.*** There are many online sources to find foreclosure listings in the Chicago area, both paid subscriptions and free. As I write this, I can tell you where to find 3,448 Friendly Foreclosure prospects in the Chicago metropolitan and suburban area just from a quick search of a popular foreclosure listing service. I can find their names, their home address, what they owe their mortgage lender, and what Zillow thinks their home is worth. I can also determine, sometimes, if they have FHA, VA, Fannie Mae, or Freddie Mac mortgages. These are 3,448 prospective Friendlies whose homes are currently scheduled to be sold at an auction. About 97% of those homes are scheduled for the Auction within the next 90 days.

One specific site I would recommend is the Illinois Foreclosure Listing Services, or "ILFLS," at **www.ilfls.com**. It's as important to a Chicago area foreclosure investor as the Multiple Listing Service, or MLS, is to a Chicago area real estate broker. The cost is nominal compared to the return on even one transaction. It's a tool of the trade you must have to thrive in the business. Auctioneer sites or foreclosure firms representing the bank are other great sources, as they often list foreclosure sales as soon as they have been scheduled – which in Illinois is a minimum of 45 days before the sale; a small window of time but these sites are a great resource.

What if you don't live in the Chicago area? Perform a Google search for something similar in your area. Alternatively, you don't have to be overly concerned about proximity with Foreclosure Friendly investments. If I lived in Milwaukee, Wisconsin, or Gary, Indiana, I would not hesitate to invest in good Foreclosure Friendlies in the Chicago area.

Chapter 9: ForeclosureFriendlies.com

3. ***Use this Book.*** If you hear about or find a home in foreclosure, perhaps on ILFLS, that looks particularly exciting to you, knock on the door and drop off a copy of this book with a polite note or card inside saying something to the effect of:

> Dear Steve, I hope this book will be of interest to you. Please have a look at Chapter Three and let me know if I may be of any assistance.
>
> Laura
> (847) 123-4567
> Laura@gmail.com

Make sure you write your name, telephone number, and email address on the inside cover.

This suggestion may sound self-serving, and it may appear to be a thinly disguised ruse to sell more books. While I hope to sell many books, that's not why I suggest this strategy. When I first became interested in buying foreclosures decades ago, I tried knocking on doors to introduce myself to engage the owners in a conversation that would result in my purchasing the home and renting it back to them… doing something similar to what I'm proposing in this book. That was a futile and discouraging effort, and I don't recommend it to anyone. The homeowners did not like me, trust me, or want to talk to me. They were also upset at my brash attempt to seemingly try to rip them off. Letters didn't work any better than door knocking.

I wish I would have had this book back then to hand to interesting Foreclosure Friendlies. Now you do! The book is an informative, inexpensive gift for the homeowner. It will explain the program for you and give you credibility. It won't require you to impose on their time or try to talk them into anything on their front doorstep. The book will clearly illustrate the benefits for them, and you won't have to "sell" anything. If they're interested and able, after they understand the program, they'll contact you. If not, you haven't made a significant investment of time or money into that prospect. A couple of days after you've left the book, try contacting them to find out if they read the book. If they haven't gotten to it yet, tell them you would like to chat after they've read it and understand how they might be able to save their home. Tell them you don't want to bother them until that time and ask them when it would be best to check back with them. It's a low pressure, good credibility approach.

If you think using the book won't be an effective tactic, don't use it. If you can find Friendlies or Investors without using a copy of this book, then my purpose has been served.

4. *Use Social Media.* Reach out on social media to those in foreclosure who are financially capable and would like to keep their homes. Let people know you're a Friendly Foreclosure Investor looking for Friendlies who might benefit from your assistance. Use some imagination and do your own marketing. Please be careful not to embarrass anyone on social media who may be in foreclosure.

Keep in mind potential Friendlies don't know you, like you, or trust you. So, be gentle and try not to be a bother to them. Their life has more than enough aggravation and stress in it right now, without your adding to it. Hopefully, the book and your personal style will provide credibility and dispel their initial distrust. In the book, I recommend Friendlies who are looking for Investors to first contact the person who left them this book. Hopefully, they'll have to look no further.

Chapter 9: ForeclosureFriendlies.com

Summary

During good economic times, foreclosure rates hover around half of 1%. That means at any time, your small town of 10,000 people probably has at least 50 people in foreclosure. As much as they would like, those homeowners in foreclosure can't hide that fact. It's generally public information. Are any of those formerly unemployed or financially distressed homeowners now recovered from their financial difficulties, and perhaps re-employed or done with their divorce or other problems? Yes, of course. Can you find those people? Yes, of course. Try some of the methods suggested here or figure out your own. Friendlies are out there in big numbers, and you can find them.

Of course, keep an eye on ForeclosureFriendlies.com. Those registered as Friendlies will be your very best leads. They should understand the program and be anxious to talk to a capable Investor.

Chapter 9: ForeclosureFriendlies.com

Like Match.com for Friendlies & Investors

As of this writing, ForeclosureFriendlies.com is a new and growing matchmaking website. It will take some time to populate fully. Please go to the website, subscribe, and create your profile.

Comparable to Match.com, the dating website, the purpose of ForeclosureFriendlies.com is to match Friendlies and Investors, so that both can live happily ever after! Completing a Friendly Foreclosure transaction can truly be a financial life event for Friendly and Investor.

Like Match.com, you can provide a little or a lot of information about yourself. Like Match.com, it will help to be friendly and forthright in your ForeclosureFriendlies.com profile. The more information you provide, the more interested partners you'll attract.

Make sure your profile provides a convenient way to contact you, either through the website or by email, text, or phone, and that you respond promptly to messages. If you're concerned about privacy, communicate only through the website or create a new email address to use only for this purpose. That will be an easy way to quickly determine how many inquiries you've received. Just remember to check it regularly!

I'm hopeful about the success of the website, but it will take some time to populate. Don't be discouraged if there are no Friendlies listed in your area. You'll find lots of opportunities to locate Friendly Homeowners or Friendly Investors online and elsewhere in life. So, search for and find those potential teammates. Gift them a copy of this book and direct them to the website so they can learn the concept from a source other than yourself. Use your imagination and work hard to find a good potential partner. Completing a Friendly Foreclosure transaction may take some work, but the results could be financially life-changing!

Friendlies and Investors should both "Have Skin in the Game. Originally, my concept was to make the ForeclosureFriendlies.com website a subscription site for Friendly Investors and a free site for Friendly Homeowners. After all, the Friendly Homeowners are the ones with financial problems. However, to make subscriptions free would allow any homeowners to register, regardless of how committed they are to keeping their home, or how financially capable they are of doing so. Paid subscriptions genuinely demonstrate the desire and the financially qualified traits required of good Friendlies. If you are sincerely interested in keeping your home and can demonstrate you're financially capable of doing so, the modest fees for registration on this website will be insignificant and should provide the best opportunity for you to find a strong Investor who understands this program and wants to help you keep your home.

Finally, Friendlies, beware of conventional foreclosure investors. Investors unfamiliar with the Foreclosure Friendly concept aren't typically looking at the Friendly Homeowner's property because they want to help the homeowner. Typically, they want to help themselves. One of the biggest risks for these investors is the fact they're usually not allowed to inspect foreclosure properties before the auction. They have little or no idea about the condition of the property. They don't know if the homeowner has recently or ever remodeled the kitchen or bathrooms. They don't know if the basement is finished, or if it is, how well it was done, or if it ever floods. Some of the bolder investors will walk around the property or knock on the homeowner's door after they learn they're in foreclosure.

Chapter 9: ForeclosureFriendlies.com

They want to know if someone lives there, and if the utilities are on, and if there's heat in the home during the winter. They also want to get a look at the interior, and they may use all kinds of stories to get people to invite them in so they can have a better look.

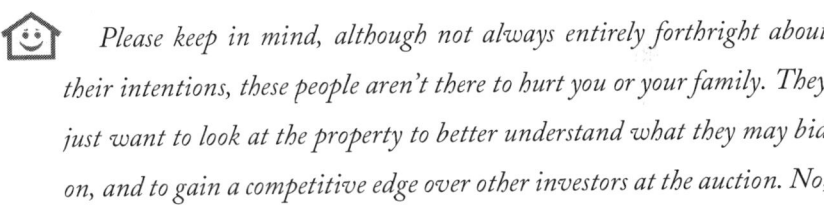 Please keep in mind, although not always entirely forthright about their intentions, these people aren't there to hurt you or your family. They just want to look at the property to better understand what they may bid on, and to gain a competitive edge over other investors at the auction. No, I don't like this practice, either, but beware, it is common.

If you want to keep your home, I recommend working only with Investors who are familiar with, and mention by name, the Foreclosure Friendly strategy. Be leery of those contacting you about your home if they are unfamiliar with the Foreclosure Friendly term or if they did not contact you via ForeclosureFriendlies.com.

Summary

The website, ForeclosureFriendlies.com, is a website designed to match Friendlies and Investors. It's a good place to find your Friendly or Investor. Keep in mind there may be healthy competition for good Friendlies and Investors on this website. If you use other methods to find your Friendlies or Investors, there may be less or no competition to complete those transactions. Competition may or may not be a good thing for you.

Chapter 10: The Amazing LIRP

Have you heard about the LIRP? LIRP is an acronym for Life Insurance Retirement Plan. What could possibly sound more boring? Nothing, but that's completely misleading. The best description I've heard is this: A LIRP is like a self-directed Roth IRA on steroids!

- It's a tax-advantaged retirement plan with no limits on contributions.
- It's a life insurance policy and possibly a long-term care insurance policy.
- It's your private bank whenever you need a loan on terrific terms, including loan payments only when and if you feel like it.
- It's all those things at the same time!

The LIRP is an exciting program you should know about whether you're in your 60s and thinking about retirement or in your 20s and just starting in the work world or any age in between.

Since reading Haroldsen on RE, I've not encountered any topic nearly as exciting as real estate... until the LIRP! I first encountered LIRPs during a presentation at a local real estate investor meeting. I was curious, so I bought a book, *Money, Wealth, Life Insurance* by Jake Thompson, and I couldn't put it down! Fortunately, it was only 61 pages, so I didn't need to put it down.

Like déjà vu, I quickly read about a dozen more books on the subject, took the required class, sat for the Illinois state exam, became a licensed insurance agent, and got my very own LIRP. **And it truly is amazing.** Less than a year later, I used my LIRP to buy a terrific Foreclosure Friendly home which yielded a 34% ROI in just 2 ½ months. I had become my own bank for Foreclosure Friendlies and any other personal investments of interest.

Under some less common circumstances, a LIRP might also provide a path for the Friendly to end a foreclosure. The LIRP could be used as a Friendly's personal bank to provide funds to reinstate the mortgage, which means pay all amounts currently past due and end the foreclosure. This method works best for homes with equity. If large enough, the Friendly might use the LIRP to buy their own home back at a substantial discount at the auction.

When asked "Why doesn't everyone use a LIRP?" author Bryan Bloom, CPA, explained that everyone who understands the LIRP does use it. That might be a slight exaggeration on Mr. Bloom's part, but there's nothing quite like a LIRP. The benefits are unparalleled.

Initially, I had intended this book to be about Foreclosure Friendlies and LIRPs. Unfortunately, that was just too much information for me to cram between the covers of one book in any digestible fashion. Although this book doesn't include a complete explanation, I couldn't help but mention the LIRP because it could be a way for more Investors to help more families save more homes. It might also be a way for Foreclosure Friendlies to end their own foreclosure nightmare or avoid financial distress in the future. So, for now, I'll leave you with a LIRP reading list and this advice:

- If you're an investor, the following book list can show you how LIRPs can be utilized simultaneously as a retirement plan, an insurance policy, and your own bank for financing Foreclosure Friendlies and anything else. Can your 401K or IRA do that? No, not nearly as well as a LIRP can.

Chapter 10: The Amazing LIRP

- If you're a homeowner in foreclosure, first and foremost, tend to the foreclosure business at hand. Don't get distracted! Later, after you've saved your home, come back to this reading list. It might help you stay out of foreclosure or financial trouble in the future. It might also help transform you from a Foreclosure Friendly homeowner into a Foreclosure Friendly Investor!

The following list is in the order I recommend reading the books[8]. Don't do anything about the LIRP until you've finished reading at least the first book on the list. As you can see, most are short books, so it's not a daunting reading list:

- *Money, Wealth, Life Insurance* by Jake Thompson – 61 pages
- *The Power of Zero* by David McKnight – 90 pages
- *Becoming Your Own Banker* by R. Nelson Nash – 92 pages
- *Look Before You LIRP* by David McKnight – 84 pages
- *Live Your Life Insurance* by Kim Butler – 75 pages
- *Confessions of a CPA: Why What I Was Taught To Be True Has Turned Out Not To Be* by Bryan Bloom – 96 Pages
- *Confessions of a CPA: The Truth about Life Insurance* by Bryan Bloom – 119 pages
- *Confessions of a CPA: The Capital Equivalent Value of Life Insurance* by Bryan Bloom – 77 pages
- *Busting the Life Insurance Lies* by Kim Butler and Jack Burns – 174 pages

---

[8] If you need a break after reading a bunch of LIRP books, sneak in something completely different: Rich Dad Poor Dad by Robert Kiyosaki – 195 pages. Kiyosaki has a unique (and I believe accurate) definition of "Rich." If combined with a LIRP strategy, Mr. Kiyosaki's suggestions about how to become "Rich" could be immensely improved.

- *Bank on Yourself* by Pamela Yellen – 225 pages
- *The Bank on Yourself Revolution* by Pamela Yellen – 279 Pages

Whether Investor or Friendly, it doesn't take long to learn about the LIRP, and it may be a financial windfall for you now or in the future. If you decide to get a LIRP, make sure your LIRP:

- Is from a large, well-respected, financially secure Mutual Life Insurance Company.
- Is NOT a MEC.
- Has a Non-Direct Loan Recognition Dividend paying policy.

Beyond these undebatable prerequisites, find a good insurance agent to get a good LIRP.

Conclusion

The Foreclosure Friendly process can save homes for families in foreclosure when foreclosure defense, mediation, bankruptcy, and loan modification efforts have failed. When successful, the Foreclosure Friendly strategy will result in the former homeowner staying in the home while leasing it at an affordable monthly rent, with an option to re-purchase it at the market value.

In addition to the improvement in the monthly payments and the future amount due on the house, if re-purchased, the former owner's family will not have to move out of the home and will continue to occupy it through the entire process. The children will continue to attend the same school, play in the same neighborhood, and sleep in their same rooms. The benefits are far more than just financial, but the economic benefits for the homeowner range from attractive to extraordinary.

Because of the immediate and uninterrupted rent receipts, the reduction or elimination of repairs and renovation expenses, and the slashed selling costs, the Foreclosure Friendly Investor profits will be an estimated 15 percentage points higher than conventional investors who buy foreclosure properties to fix and flip. The average value of foreclosure auction properties where I reside is currently about $165,000. In my area, on average, an Investor should achieve profits of almost $25,000 more with a Friendly Foreclosure transaction than with a conventional foreclosure property investment. The risk of a Friendly Foreclosure investment is also far lower than the risk of a conventional foreclosure auction fix and flip, in which there are a multitude of unknown variables. Note also that coming to the aid of families in desperate need provides Foreclosure Friendly Investors with far more than just financial rewards.

The LIRP, described only briefly in this book, provides Investors with an attractive means to finance their Friendly Foreclosure transactions. That's the primary reason I included the discussion in this book. However, the LIRP also provides Friendlies with an opportunity to safeguard themselves from financial distress in the future, and perhaps gradually transform themselves from a Foreclosure Friendly Homeowner to a Foreclosure Friendly Investor.

The purpose of this book is to illustrate the significant financial benefits of the Foreclosure Friendly strategy for both Friendlies and Investors. The companion website, ForeclosureFriendlies.com, is intended to bring Friendlies and Investors together when they cannot otherwise find each other.

Friendlies, I wish you the best of luck in your efforts to save your homes. Investors, I hope you make a fortune helping a multitude of nice families keep their treasured abodes. Please let me know if I can assist.

POSTSCRIPT I — So, You Want to Invest in Real Estate?

This section is for those who are intrigued by the Foreclosure Friendly strategy but know little or nothing about real estate. For those readers, it would be wise to learn a bit about real estate before diving in. This section assumes you know nothing about real estate, which is where I started when I read my first book on the topic. So, Rookies:

Step 1. Read 'til you Bleed!

If you're thinking about becoming a real estate investor, start by reading up. **Many good books describe different methods to evaluate, acquire, manage, and profit from real estate investing.** Read them all! I did, or at least I tried to! My eyes were probably bloodshot for a year from all that reading.

You can be a flipper, which means buying and selling properties quickly, or you can be a holder, which means buying and holding properties for long-term rentals or retirement income. You can invest in single family homes or multi-family buildings or retail or commercial or industrial or land or options. If reading Haroldsen on RE has the same effect on you as it did on me, you'll want to read everything else about real estate you can get your hands on, and that's not a bad idea. There are many good books written by authors with decades of experience. They will give you valuable advice to help avoid the multitude of mistakes the authors made along the way.

The book you're reading now is important, but it will focus on only one tiny part of the real estate investment arena: Friendly Foreclosures. That is not the only real estate investment about which I recommend you become familiar. Yes, Friendly Foreclosures can be exciting and profitable. They also have a unique philanthropic edge, but if you like real estate, they are by no means the only investments about which you should become familiar.

Regardless of which areas of real estate you pursue, I recommend starting slowly, patiently, and inexpensively. OK, skip the slowly part! Act quickly on the study and preparation part, but don't invest in properties too quickly. You have a lot of reading and much work to do before you buy your first property. However, don't worry—you're not going to spend the next couple of years reading books on the subject before you invest. Start on Step 2 immediately while working through Step 1.

During this preparation stage, please don't run out and buy the first multi-unit residential property you find with a For Sale sign in the window. While you are gearing up to become a real estate investor, you will discover many real estate opportunities along the way. There are, literally, millions of them out there. People will tell you that you had better make an offer quick! "Otherwise, it will likely be sold to someone else by Friday!" Don't be taken in by that type of negotiation and persuasion tactic. Please understand and remember:

THE DEAL OF A LIFETIME IN REAL ESTATE COMES ALONG ABOUT ONCE A MONTH!

If someone else buys that incredible property you're looking at today, don't worry. Next month an even better one will come up, and you'll be happy you didn't buy the first one. My long-time friends are probably sick of hearing me say that, but they all know it's true, and yes, I say it a lot!

Postscript I

Step 2. Get your Real Estate Broker License

Different states have different regulations and requirements for the licensed practice of real estate. As mentioned earlier, I'm a licensed Illinois Managing Real Estate Broker, or a "managing broker." Since obtaining my managing broker license years ago, I've maintained it for investment purposes. Being licensed allows me to take (or save) real estate commissions when buying or selling my properties. Having a real estate license also allows me membership in the local Multiple Listing Service, the "MLS." Access to the MLS is essential for active, single-family residential investors, like me.

No, I don't drive people around on weekends to show them homes to buy, and I don't take listings from people wishing to sell their homes. However, one of my first jobs in real estate was doing just that, and **I had more fun selling homes than any job I've had since.** Don't be afraid to try real estate sales if you have an interest in a sales profession. Real estate sales can be a lucrative and enjoyable career. It helps if you have a working spouse or partner, or substantial savings or investments which can provide health insurance and benefits and help you survive real estate market downturns, which will happen from time to time, but you'll definitely have some fun!

Real Estate Broker, "Broker," versus Sponsoring or Managing Real Estate Broker, "Managing Broker," in Illinois. There are specific regulations regarding the practice of real estate brokerage and the payment of commissions in Illinois. Only a managing broker may receive or pay commissions to brokers, who must have a license under a managing broker. Brokers versus managing brokers is a critical distinction because only managing brokers in Illinois can collect sales commissions. Then they split the commission, perhaps 50/50, under a written agreement with their selling broker. As a real estate investor in Illinois, you will probably want to become a managing broker, but that is not mandatory. Being a broker, but not a managing broker, can also work, depending on your circumstances.

If you're interested in obtaining an Illinois broker or managing broker license, feel free to visit my **Real Estate School of Northern Illinois** at www.RESNIL.com. We have pre-licensing and continuing education online and classroom courses available. If you become a student in one of my classes, please introduce yourself and let me know what you think of this book.

Step 3. Buy, Don't Rent, Your Own Home with No Money Down

There are several ways to buy homes or investment property with no money down. Most are risky and unduly expensive.

Installment contracts for deed, owner financing, and quiet assumptions are the most common structures for little or no-money down deals in Illinois. All are risky for buyers and sellers. When considering any variation of these transactions, both buyer and seller should consult a qualified real estate attorney.

The more straightforward, safer approach to buying a home with no money down is to:

1. Get your managing broker license or broker license with a real estate office that will allow you to keep 99% of the office commission for your own purchase(s) and sale(s). Get pre-qualified or pre-approved for an FHA, VA, or any other mortgage with a low-down payment.

Postscript I

2. Use the MLS to find a suitable home with a 6% or higher total commission, with at least half of the commission payable to the buyer's broker (you!). You want at least a 3% commission payable to you, the buyer's broker.

3. The 3% commission plus favorable prorations, such as real estate taxes in Illinois, will hopefully cover the entire down payment and closing costs. If not, ask for additional concessions when you make the purchase offer on the home, such as repairs and decorating credits or closing costs credits.

If closing costs in your area are high or not favorable to buyers and you can't do a no money down deal with only a 3% commission, then confine your search to homes on which you can take a 5%–7% commission, such as

- For Sale by Owners, "FSBOs"
- Expired and canceled listings
- Sales that have "fallen through"

With the above options, you should be able to negotiate a good commission from the seller. With an FHA or similar loan with a 3½% down payment, you will almost certainly be able to purchase that property with no money down, given the higher commission payable to you.

I purchased my first home with an FHA mortgage and a 3% commission. Given favorable real estate tax prorations in Illinois, I had no net purchase costs and received a check for about $300 at the closing table. My second home was a similar transaction. My third home purchase was a house for which the prior sales contract had fallen through just days earlier. I acted quickly, offered the owner his full asking price, and took a

7% commission. The seller was so, so happy, as was my family. That's an easy no money down deal in any area.

Pessimists will rationalize that only undesirable or overpriced homes don't sell or have listings that are canceled or expired, but they would be wrong. That thought process is particularly inaccurate for FSBOs and the multitude of deals that fall through due to buyer inability to close. My third home, mentioned above, is pictured on the cover of this book. To my knowledge, this property has never been in foreclosure. It is simply a good example of the quality of home you can acquire with No Money Down.

How valuable was my real estate license to me? During the 10+ years living in those three homes, my home equity grew from zero dollars to six figures. That's not an unusually high amount of home equity growth over that period.

Absent my managing broker license, I probably would have been renting rather than owning homes, thereby never accumulating any home equity. Renting was the standard for my family when I grew up. Furthermore, when I was just beginning my work career, I had no chance of saving that "20% down payment" which was all I knew about buying a home before reading Haroldsen on RE.

In summary, I purchased my first three homes using none of my own money. Instead, I used my real estate commissions, a couple of FHA mortgages, and profits from the sales of my prior homes. Buying these homes with no money down was a fun and surprisingly easy process.

If you want to become a real estate investor, **get your Real Estate Broker license!**

POSTSCRIPT II – Yes, We Can Help You!

If you like the Friendly Foreclosure idea but are nervous about how to do it… we can help!

If you're a Foreclosure Friendly Homeowner, it's only natural to be nervous right now. Get yourself a good attorney! This is too big and too important for a do-it-yourself project. Don't go it alone. Get a professional. Do that for your family! If you're in the Chicago metropolitan or suburban area, feel free to contact my office for legal assistance.

If foreclosure defense, mediation, loan modification applications, and bankruptcy couldn't save your home, you don't have many other, if any, good options left. This strategy can only help you. Nothing you do with this strategy should shorten your stay in your home or make matters worse for you, and you shouldn't spend much money if the effort fails. So, learn the concept, embrace it, and get to work!

If you used an attorney when you bought your home, that might be a good person to call right now. You probably derived confidence from using that attorney previously. We strongly recommend using one for your Friendly Foreclosure transaction. An attorney can offer assurance that your Friendly Foreclosure transaction will be handled properly. The attorney won't guarantee success, as nobody can, but you'll be giving it your best shot.

If you're an Investor, I also recommend using an attorney, particularly to review the condition of title before bidding at the auction. Mistakes in that area can be financially devastating.

Following is a summary of services my firm offers to assist with Friendly Foreclosure transactions.

For Foreclosure Friendly Homeowners in the Chicago area, we may:

- Assist in identifying and vetting an Investor.
- Represent you in the lease/purchase transaction with the Investor.
- Represent you, if need be, in the foreclosure case.
- Evaluate and assist with a bankruptcy, which may give you more time.

For Investors in the Chicago area, we may:

- Represent you in transactions with Foreclosure Friendly Homeowners.
- Represent you in conventional purchase, sale, or short sale transactions.
- Assist you with a LIRP.

For Illinois residents outside of our Chicagoland service area, we would consider providing various services on a case by case basis.

For residents outside of Illinois, we cannot act as your attorney in any capacity. However, we can help you with a LIRP anywhere in the U.S.

Finally, we can help anyone interested in becoming a licensed Illinois Real Estate Broker. Just visit our website for the Real Estate School of Northern Illinois at www.RESNIL.com.

POSTSCRIPT III – Bankers, Increase Foreclosure Recovery Revenue by Decreasing Auction Bids!

As I've done elsewhere in this book, I'll use the term bank or banker in this section to represent the bank, lender, mortgage servicer, mortgage owner, and foreclosure plaintiff interchangeably.

This is a standalone section aimed at banking personnel who would like to reduce costs and increase profits for their bank. By modifying the auction bidding strategy, bankers have substantial opportunity to do this in the foreclosure arena. I hope banks will contact me to arrange a trial, whereby they put my assertions to the test. I'm happy to prove it to you! With a reasonable sample size, we should be able to prove the benefits of lower, pre-announced auction bids quickly. I believe bankers will be amazed at the results of such an experiment. So, if you're involved in setting opening bids for auctions, please give me a call.

Not long ago, banks nearly always bid the full judgment amount due from the homeowner at foreclosure auctions in Illinois. That's why banks won most of those auctions. Today, in Illinois, they tend to bid less than the full amount due, but they still win the auctions about 65% of the time. Unfortunately for banks, winning at auctions means losing after the auctions. They're terrible at selling homes! Banks are good at many things, but selling homes isn't one of them. Banks recover about 50% of the market value of homes (if they were in decent condition), and it takes them about a year after the auction to do so in Illinois. That's horrendous performance, and below is how they do it.

$100,000	100% fair market value in reasonable condition (highly unlikely)
12 Months	Time from auction to gain possession, market, re-sell, and close
$18,000	1.5%/Month holding costs and time value of money between the auction and re-sale
$5,000	5% Minimum costs for cleaning and repairs to market the home
$11,000	10% to 12% Closing costs upon re-sale (in Illinois)
$16,000	15% to 20% Reduced sale price due to foreclosure stigma, poor condition, and undesirable bank sale terms such as As-Is, No Warranties, and No Survey.
$50,000	50% Total bank recovery

Bankers can debate the magnitude of the costs listed above, but there's no reason to do so. Bank costs are actually much higher. In addition to those hard cost estimates above, banks have other considerable overhead and expenses.

An REO, the bank acronym for Real Estate Owned, is a property acquired by the bank at the foreclosure auction or otherwise. Banks must keep a staff of property managers, real estate broker liaisons, contract negotiators, closing agents, attorneys, and the corporate facilities and support staff and overhead that go with REO personnel.

Whether banks outsource or handle those responsibilities in-house, they amount to a substantial cost. I can't give you a close estimate on those related costs, but bankers know they're fortunate if their average net recovery is 50% of fair market value on foreclosed properties when considering all related expenses.

So, bankers, this is my proposal:

1. Place all auction bids at 65% of your estimated market value of the home.

2. Post your opening bids on a publicly accessible website well before the auction. Investors don't shop at auctions like they do at Walmart. They need time and research to properly evaluate which homes they pursue at auctions. If they know the price in advance, and if it seems right, they'll do the research and come to the auction prepared to bid. If they know your bank always bids 65% of your estimated fair market value, they'll keep an eye out for auctions with your properties. If your properties and future opening bids are published well in advance on a public website, that will be a tremendous boost to your auction sales and foreclosure recoveries. It will also create investor attention and bidding competition for your properties.

The result of adopting the proposed auction bidding strategy would drastically increase the number of your foreclosure properties selling to investors at auctions. Foreclosure Friendly Investors may certainly be willing to go as high as 70% of market value, and sometimes higher, so they will consistently outbid your 65% starting bid. There will also be more competitive conventional auction bidding on your properties. As calculated earlier in this book, conventional real estate investors need to buy auction properties for 65% or less of the estimated finished market value to make a profit.

Your new bidding policy could increase your net recovery on auction properties from 50% to over 65% of the estimated market value on most of your auction properties. That's better than a 30% increase in your recovery, i.e., a $65,000 recovery on a $100,000 property rather than a $50,000 recovery is a $15,000 increase which is 30% above the $50,000 expected recovery. Moreover, you'll make that improved recovery shortly after the auction rather than a year after.

With this policy shift, you'll also be able to re-deploy much of your considerable REO related personnel and support resources to more productive and profitable endeavors, thereby further reducing costs and increasing productivity.

Finally, by taking a more profitable approach to your bidding practices, you'll be acting in the best financial interests of your bank while helping some of your distressed clients save their homes. You'll also be enhancing your reputation in the process.

Please consider this favorable adjustment to your auction bidding strategy. If you adopt the suggested approach, I'll provide you with plenty of praise and publicity on my website and in the next edition of this book. Investors will get the word quickly and keep a sharp eye on any foreclosure properties with your mortgage loans. Your foreclosure properties will garner much attention and interest, which will have a positive effect on the number sold and the prices garnered at auction.

In addition, you would be doing a massive service to your defaulted mortgage clients, while improving your profits, and your reputation. Thanks for considering, and please contact me if I may be of any assistance in this endeavor, or if you would like to discuss a trial run.

Acknowledgment

The person most responsible for bringing this book and its sister website from the dark crevices of my mind to the light of day has been my long-time Operations Manager, Katie-Lee Harrison.  In addition to her considerable daily duties of running our law firm, Katie-Lee has acted as proofreader, editor, formatter, website designer, art and literary critic, publishing agent, muse and more. She's one of a kind, and this project could not have been completed in this decade without her inspiration and commitment. Thanks, Katie-Lee, for your endless talents and energy and your unfailing loyalty.

Made in the USA
Columbia, SC
17 January 2019